Mansfield Park

Isobel Armstrong has been Professor of English at the University of Southampton since 1979. She was educated at the Friends' School, Saffron Walden, and graduated from Leicester University. She has taught at the universities of London, Leicester and Princeton. She is the author of *Victorian Scrutinies* (Athlone, 1972), Victorian reviews of poetry, and *Language as Living Form in 19th Century Poetry* (Harvester, 1982), a study of Romantic and Victorian poetic language in the light of Hegelian philosophy. She has also published the *Routledge Critical History of Victorian Poetry* and, in addition to editing a volume of Victorian women poets, she is embarking on work on gender, language and politics in the Romantic period which includes a study of the novel.

Penguin Critical Studies
Advisory Editor: Bryan Loughrey

Jane Austen

Mansfield Park

Isobel Armstrong

Penguin Books

PENGUIN BOOKS

Published by the Penguin Group
Penguin Books Ltd, 27 Wrights Lane, London W8 5TZ, England
Penguin Books USA Inc., 375 Hudson Street, New York, New York 10014, USA
Penguin Books Australia Ltd, Ringwood, Victoria, Australia
   Penguin Books Canada Ltd, 10 Alcorn Avenue, Toronto, Ontario, Canada M4V 3B2
Penguin Books (NZ) Ltd, 182–190 Wairau Road, Auckland 10, New Zealand

Penguin Books Ltd, Registered Offices: Harmondsworth, Middlesex, England

First published 1988
10 9 8 7 6 5

Copyright © Isobel Armstrong, 1988
All rights reserved

Made and printed in Great Britain by
Clays Ltd, St Ives plc
Filmset in Monophoto Times

Contents

Acknowledgements

I am grateful to the following for advice and help: my mother, Marjorie Hughes; my colleague Dr E. N. Millett; my typist, Alison Hamlin.

1. Introduction: The Novelist and the Novel

Until recently Jane Austen has been very easily assimilated into the canon of great writers in a way which seems to make it unnecessary to think about her gender, class and politics. The entry on Jane Austen's place in Western literature in the *Encyclopaedia Britannica*, for instance, describes her work in the following way:

As her novels grew in depth, so did Jane Austen's moral perceptions . . . She is the spokesman for sanity and intelligence and builds up positive values against which the objects of her attack can be judged. She is by no means a simple novelist: working within chosen limits, she observes and describes closely the subtleties of relationships between people. She looks continually to discover the principles of conduct that animate them, but her analysis is sympathetic as a rule and her vision is basically comic. She is a master of dialogue and writes with great economy, hardly ever wasting a word.

This is a common and in many ways sound account of Jane Austen, perceiving her to be the master of and spokesman for sanity and stable values, unconsciously assuming that the words 'master' and 'spokesman' can be used in a neutral way to denote a concern with rationality and stability. It cannot be assumed, however, that gender is unimportant for Jane Austen's work, or that the concern with stability is unconnected with it. In this study I shall explore the connection between the concern with stability and the fact that Jane Austen was writing as a woman. And this involves some consideration of the culture in which Jane Austen was writing.

First, how does the idea of stability come to be connected with Jane Austen and in particular with *Mansfield Park*? In a famous passage she wrote: '3 or 4 Families in a Country village is the very thing to work on.' This remark is often related to the closed and stable environments of the novels and their subject-matter. It is appropriate to the small town and upper-class country life with its estates and the houses of the gentry which is the setting of *Pride and Prejudice*, Jane Austen's first novel though it was not published until 1813. It is appropriate to *Northanger Abbey*, begun the year after *Pride and Prejudice* in 1797 (published 1818), which moves between town as represented by Bath and country estates. It seems particularly appropriate to *Mansfield Park* (1814), *Emma* (1815) and *Persuasion* (1818), set respectively on a country estate

1

in Northamptonshire, near the village of Highbury in Hampshire and Kellynch Hall near Lyme Regis. Rural and enclosed though they are, however, there is always an incipiently disruptive situation at the heart of the novel or an invasive energy pressing in from the outside. In *Sense and Sensibility* and *Pride and Prejudice* it is the sudden arrival of strange young men and officers from the army and the social upheaval this creates. And these two novels disclose a fragile stability at the centre of the characters' worlds. The two sisters in *Sense and Sensibility* are threatened with a fall in social status through straitened means after the death of their father. In *Pride and Prejudice* the future of the Bennet daughters and their mother is highly uncertain because their father's estate is entailed. *Mansfield Park*, seemingly the centre of security and stability, is seriously threatened financially at the start of the novel when Sir Thomas Bertram has to go to Antigua to put his estates there in order. His visit to the West Indies is lengthy and Mrs Norris speaks of an uncertain time 'when a large part of his income was unsettled'. Perhaps Emma is the most secure of Jane Austen's heroines, but even she is constantly reminded of the straitened condition of the almost distressed gentlewoman, Miss Bates, and illegitimacy enters the security of the Woodhouse household in the form of Harriet. Perhaps these elements of instability are disguised by many of the characters' own confident expectations of norms of conduct commensurate with stability. But Jane Austen is capable sometimes of giving a shock to such norms: in *Pride and Prejudice* Elizabeth's giddy sisters return from a party given by one of the officers' wives and report on the fun they had dressing an officer in women's clothes.

Jane Austen herself, the daughter of a Tory clergyman, lived a life sufficiently uneventful, perhaps, for us to believe that she was the product of stable values as well as someone who endorsed and explored them in her novels. Born in 1775 at the village of Steventon in Hampshire, she might be the epitome of one of those '3 or 4 Families' which she saw as the ideal material of her novels. However, for a period of eight years, the Austen family lived in a series of lodgings until they settled at Chawton in Hampshire in 1809. Significantly, most of her major work was produced after this.

Though it would be wrong to exaggerate insecurity in Jane Austen's life, it is important to see that on the whole the characters of her novels are often luckier, richer and of higher social status than she was. However, though the gap between her fiction and her life must be registered, it is undoubtedly the case that she occupied a comparatively privileged world, a world where 'Families' meant upper-class families and not those of the poor, a world which was connected with influential circles. Her life could not have been more different from that of her anti-type, Mrs Elizabeth Inchbald, the authoress whom she covertly introduces at the heart of *Mansfield Park*, like an explosive presence, at one of its morally most crucial points, the performance of *Lovers' Vows*. Mrs Inchbald was the adapter and rewriter of this play by the German playwright Kotzebue. Twenty years or so older than Jane Austen and one of five daughters of a Roman Catholic family living in Bury St Edmunds, she was bewitched with the theatre. She took flight to London to pursue an acting and writing career, at one time taking walk-on parts to support herself. She married an actor and continued to write, eventually achieving fame and even comparative wealth, which seems to have gone to the support of needy relations. Though she left £6,000 at her death, she ended her life in comparative hardship, waiting on herself and carrying domestic water supplies up three flights of stairs. It is not known whether or not Jane Austen knew of this while she was writing *Mansfield Park*. Mrs Inchbald outlived her by just four years. But the most important aspect of this contrast is not the difference between the virtually declassed actress's life, with its hardship and poverty, society glamour and rather rakish renown, and the life of a Tory gentlewoman in relatively comfortable circumstances. Mrs Inchbald was ideologically at the opposite pole from Jane Austen: she publicly declared her interest in the egalitarian and social ideals of the French Revolution; she was an informed devotee of Rousseau and her writing was overtly political, attacking false social ideals and the structures of privilege which created a huge gap between the rich and the poor. Some people think her radicalism sentimental; but there was no doubt that she would have represented Jacobinical elements to a Tory writer. It is fascinating that Jane Austen had the resilience to introduce her subversive antithesis into the very drawing-room of Mansfield Park, testing out the stable values being explored at one level by the text and enabling them to be interrogated by another female writer. This silent dialogue with Mrs Inchbald, of which more will be said later, suggests that the stability of Jane Austen's environments is being explored and negotiated in a complex way and is never taken for granted by the text. We can begin to see what this has to do with the question of gender by looking more closely at the novel and some of the debates in which it is participating with other texts written around the same time.

As so many critics have remarked, *Mansfield Park* is a nineteenth-century Cinderella story. The novel begins with the decision of Sir Thomas Bertram to take his niece Fanny Price into his household and to bring her up. His wife's sister has made an improvident marriage and appeals for help. The decision is made at the instigation of another sister-in-law, Mrs Norris, who increasingly comes to take the position of a surrogate wife and mother to his children. It is an ambiguous decision from the start, as Mrs Norris herself actually relies on a vicarious generosity and has no intention of being responsible for Fanny, though she implies that she will be at some future time. The integrity of Sir Thomas ensures that Fanny is brought to Mansfield Park and she arrives, shy and terrified: 'Mrs Price seemed rather surprised that a girl should be fixed on, when she had so many fine boys, but accepted the offer most thankfully'.

Fanny is given an insensitive welcome by the arrogant and overconfident Bertram sisters, Maria, the eldest, and Julia. Lady Bertram, who remains passive and inactive throughout the novel, devoted only to her dogs, treats Fanny with well-meaning politeness but she has resigned her power and duties to Mrs Norris long ago. Tom, the elder brother, who is occupied in doing what elder brothers in upper-class families traditionally do – getting into debt and living a dissolute life (which brings serious illness upon him later in the novel) – teases Fanny perfunctorily. It is only Edmund, the younger son, destined for the church, who genuinely understands Fanny's homesickness and befriends her, acting as her guide and protector. In fact, he is her teacher as well as her friend: 'he made reading useful by talking to her of what she read, and heightened its attraction by judicious praise. In return for such services she loved him better than anybody in the world except William; her heart was divided between the two.'

William is Fanny's brother, who is helped to a position in the navy by Sir Thomas, but apart from brief visits from him Fanny grows up entirely exposed to the formative influence of Mansfield Park. But the mood and moral tone of Mansfield Park seem to change in exact relation to the absence of the patriarchal figure, Sir Thomas. The worsening of his financial interests in Antigua (it is worth mentioning that Jane Austen's father had connections with Antigua) forces him to go to the West Indies. During his absence Fanny's situation as a dependent relation worsens and her status in the household becomes more insecure when two visitors with London connections arrive to stay with the Grants – Dr Grant holds the living near Mansfield Park. These are the brother and sister Henry and Mary Crawford. They disrupt the household in many ways. Fanny watches herself being displaced in Edmund's affections by Mary, even to the extent of seeing her ride the horse Edmund had specially obtained for Fanny herself. Henry flirts with Julia and Maria, a particularly notable indiscretion since Maria has become engaged to Mr Rushworth, the rich but silly heir to a neighbouring estate. Mary flirts with Edmund despite her lack of sympathy for his decision to become a clergyman. All the flirtations become more advanced when the group visits Mr Rushworth's estate, and they become even more complex when, with Tom's return and the addition of a London fop, Mr Yates, they decide to act the *risqué* play *Lovers' Vows*. Fanny intransigently refuses to act though she helps the players with their lines. With the unexpected arrival of Sir Thomas the play is terminated.

In fact, the play is a rehearsal for everything else that happens in the book. Fanny, intransigent at eighteen, remains so, resisting the importunate proposals of Henry during an unquiet visit to her family in Portsmouth, and refusing to marry him despite the pressure put on her by Sir Thomas. Maria elopes with Henry, who has become bored with waiting for Fanny, and Julia elopes with the egregious Mr Yates. When it is clear to Edmund that Mary has no moral feeling about the elopement of Maria, interpreting it literally as an indiscretion and assuming that the couple might have got away with it had they eloped with less panache, Edmund falls out of love with Mary and back into love with Fanny. By this time it has become clear to the Mansfield Park household that Fanny is indispensable to them and the novel ends with Fanny's success. Edmund and Fanny prepare to welcome Fanny's sister, Susan, into the household and to train her in the renewed moral values of Mansfield Park.

Even from this brief summary of the novel it is clear that Jane Austen is interested in the fate of the dependent woman, the quiet, delicate Fanny, who assimilates the best values of Mansfield Park even to the extent of maintaining them more thoroughly than members of the Bertram family. It is she, one might say, who stabilizes and even refines the Bertram stock. It is interesting that it seems more natural and an easier task for the Bertram family to take Fanny into their midst rather than a boy, despite the risk, seen clearly by Sir Thomas and Mrs Norris at the start of the novel, of marriage between cousins. To understand this it is useful to return for a moment to Mrs Inchbald, Jane Austen's anti-type.

In 1796 Mrs Inchbald published a novel called *Nature and Art*. It was the year Jane Austen began the novel which was to become *Pride and Prejudice*. The novel is the story of two brothers and their sons. The more successful of the brothers becomes a Dean of the Church of England and receives into his house his nephew, who is orphaned. The young Henry has been brought up far away from the influences of the civilized life of Western Europe and asks his uncle some awkward questions:

'There are in society,' continued the Dean, 'rich and poor; the poor are born to serve the rich.'

'And what are the rich born for?'

'To be served by the poor.'

'But suppose the poor would not serve them?'

'Then they must starve.'

Young Henry constantly calls attention to the misapplication of words: for instance, he corrects 'war' to 'massacre' and 'compliments' to 'lies'. It is not surprising that when he marries he does not take up residence in a country seat; instead, he and his wife were 'the thankful inhabitants of a small house, or hut, placed on the edge of the sea'. More striking than the material contrast between the fates of Fanny and Henry are the different choices open to Fanny as a woman: it is not even that love in a hut is not enough for Fanny or Jane Austen; it is that Fanny can only either live at Mansfield Park or return to the noisy and uncomfortable household at Portsmouth. There are many reasons for her ductile and 'conforming' behaviour (Ch. 2), but one of them is that it was a necessity for her to be so. This may have been behind the decision to take a girl into the Mansfield Park household rather than one of Mrs Price's 'fine boys'. It was a prudent decision even while it carried obligations, which Sir Thomas at least recognizes. Twice he finds himself obliged to take responsibility for her even when he had not really expected to have to do so. He finds himself taking the major responsibility at first, and when he expects Mrs Norris to take Fanny to live with her, hoping that he will be relieved of providing for her in the present and assuming that Mrs Norris will leave Fanny provision for her services so that her financial future will pass from him to Mrs Norris, he is disappointed. Lady Bertram assures Mrs Norris that Fanny will be no 'encumbrance' to Mansfield Park if she stays there, but we know that Sir Thomas is in fact encumbered financially. It is a magnanimous and responsible action, but it does likewise impose obligations and limits on Fanny, even though she is the last person to be aware of this at first. Certainly, her dependent position makes it impossible for her to challenge the very basis of social arrangements in the way that Henry challenges his uncle when he asks uncomfortable questions about the poor. Henry says all that Fanny cannot say. The novel does not speak of the social arrangements upon which the privilege of Mansfield Park is based, and Fanny cannot speak of these either, because she is potentially one of the poor herself and but for Sir Thomas's generosity she would be serving the rich or starving. Indeed, there is a sense in which she is already serving the rich of

Mansfield Park, for she takes the subservient place of the dependent relation without question.

Fanny's situation at Mansfield Park is complex and it is not clear how far she or any of the characters are aware of it. It is something the reader grasps from the subtle negotiations of the text and from the unstated relationships between characters and situations disclosed as the narrative progresses. Enough has been said, however, for one to grasp a number of things about this novel. First, Fanny's social position as potentially one of the poor and her position as a woman are both important to the novel, but we arrive at these conclusions indirectly. They are not stated in the text. Secondly, the narrative strategy of the novel is delicate and inconspicuous and seems to screen and make subliminal the pressures of politics and the fact of gender. It may be that there are more of these subliminal pressures at work in the novel and that they will indicate how its complexities can be read. Where Mrs Inchbald speaks out, Jane Austen does not. But that does not mean that she was less concerned with questions which were profoundly important to her culture. I will turn to some of these, for it is by seeing how these subliminal questions can be read and understood that one can begin to approach the narrative strategies and the language of the novel.

An interesting critic of *Mansfield Park*, Tony Tanner, has described the concern with stability and security in the novel as the result of a recognition that the rural England of Jane Austen's time was undergoing major changes. He notices a number of questions covertly encountered in the novel. He highlights the transition to an industrial from a rural population going on at the time, the Peninsular War against Napoleon, the threat of the Jacobinism spread by the French Revolution and the financial interests of the Whig and Tory parties.

It might be worth reminding ourselves what England was like in the years 1811–13, the very eve of Waterloo, when Jane Austen was writing the novel. In general we can see that it was a period of great stability just about to give way to a time of unimagined changes. At that time most of the population (some thirteen million) were involved in rural and agricultural work: yet within another twenty years the majority of Englishmen became urban dwellers involved with industry, and the great railway age had begun. Throughout the early years of the century the cities were growing at a great rate; the network of canals was completed, the main roads were being remade. Regency London, in particular, boomed and became, among other things, a great centre of fashion. On the other hand, England in 1813 was still predominantly a land of country towns and villages, a land of rural routines which were scarcely touched by the seven campaigns of the

Peninsular War against Napoleon. The Prime Minister was the unremarkable Lord Liverpool and politics were still dominated by the aristocracy and landed gentry, with only a few spokesmen for the new commercial and manufacturing interests. Their main general concern was the possibility of French 'Jacobinism' spreading among the discontented lower classes in England. There was not a lot of difference between the Tory and the Whig parties. The Tory party was more conservative, almost totally opposed to any sort of popular radicalism and political reform: it was the party of the Church of England and identified itself with tradition, continuity, order and an aristocratic attachment to the land. The Whigs were a little closer to the City and business interests, and they wanted some reforms in the system of government which would lessen the power of the landed interest.

Tony Tanner uses this information to explain why *Mansfield Park* is so concerned with stability and continuity. He reads the novel as an essentially conservative work. I feel that the case is a little more problematic, but one can assent, with some reservations, to his picture of England at this time. It is a helpful picture but one should add to it a little more about the intellectual concerns circulating in England at that time. Tony Tanner is right to notice the deep-felt sense of incipient change. Some of this was created in and through the institutions which supported tradition. John Wesley's Methodist movement, for instance, sprang from the Church of England before it became a new formation in its own right. It was part of the evangelistic Christianity which had its flowering in England at the end of the eighteenth century and beyond. The apathy of the Church of England as much as any theological dispute provoked an attempt to redefine the essentials of the spiritual life. Wesley appealed to the poor, and there is no overt indication that either Dr Grant or Edmund have assimilated Methodist influence, except that Edmund's deep concern with ethical conduct certainly does not resemble the worldliness of Dr Grant. Mary taunts him with Methodism. One could say that, as with so much of Jane Austen, there is a subliminal response to new currents of thought and an attempt to negotiate them in the text of the novel. Jane Austen herself once said, rather mystifyingly, that the novel was about 'ordination'.

It was the religious impulse which was behind the growing desire to abolish the slave trade and behind the anti-slavery campaign. Sir Thomas would have been directly involved in slavery as his estates in Antigua would be founded on it and the wealth of Mansfield Park would have been created by it. It is interesting that Antigua is such a trouble-spot in the novel, a concealed, unsettling and destabilizing element, the place which calls Sir Thomas away and which is responsible for his 'unsettled' fortunes. The novel is silent about the nature of the trouble there and no character expresses political views about the source of Sir Thomas's wealth, but it is one of those subliminal issues which silently ask questions in the text, as will be seen later. Mrs Inchbald's presence in the Mansfield Park drawing-room makes us ask questions about the relation between exploitation and privilege, questions which are provoked by the text. It is almost as if the transgressions and outbreaks of unruly activity which follow Sir Thomas's departure from Mansfield Park echo a parallel outbreak of energy and rebellious feeling on his estate. And both require censorship and control. The demand for relaxation of the slave trade can be associated with those 'Jacobinical' forces which were dissolving traditional values. In the novel the privileged seem to be inadvertently in alliance with the exploited element they depend on.

Interestingly, it is the improprieties at Mansfield Park which call up speculation as to the cause of the trouble in Antigua. It is one of the screening devices so prevalent in the novel, and simply because of the uncertainty of the cause of the difficulties, the threat of trouble seems that much more sinister.

It also screens the threat of trouble nearer at home, both while Jane Austen was writing and at the time when the novel would have been set. As a result of enclosure – the appropriation of common land sanctioned by acts of parliament – the plight of the labouring poor, where the day-labourer succeeded to the small farmer, was one of unparalleled distress and poverty. Significantly, Northamptonshire, where the novel is set, was one of the most heavily enclosed areas of the Midlands. Outbreaks of rebellion and Jacobin revolutionary ideas were deeply feared at this time.

With religion, slavery and poverty, we might mention another indirect concern of the novel, and that is with education. The period Jane Austen lived through saw the most intensive speculation on the education of children and a questioning of eighteenth-century theories. The formative nature of education was well understood by her contemporary William Wordsworth, and though Fanny is not fostered alike by beauty and by fear, as Wordsworth believed himself to be, the novel's concern with education is as searching as anything in *The Prelude*. In this Jane Austen is allied with another of her anti-types, Mary Wollstonecraft, who attached great importance to the education of women and thought the inadequacy of female education was largely due to women's willingness to remain subservient to men. Of course, Jane Austen read many conservative accounts of badly educated women in contemporary novels and attended to the disquisitions on woman's duty such as are found in the work of Hannah Moore. Nevertheless, the novel's critique of women's education is oddly akin to that of a more radical writer.

The strange sense we have in *Mansfield Park* of Jane Austen as an explorer of the conservative reverse-image of so many romantic concerns is endorsed by another slightly veiled debate on the idea of nature and culture. This emerges briefly in the discussion of what seems the very reverse of Wordsworthian nature: landscape gardening. It occurs when the group are proposing to visit Mr Rushworth's estate, Sotherton. Mr Rushworth is considering 'improving' his estate by fundamentally changing it through landscaping. The different sides people take about this indicate their values. This leads us to another concern of the novel, and that is with the nature of art and its influence. That is why the performance of the play is so important. For just as the art of landscaping may be suspect, so may be the influence of the play and its artifice.

But there is now a question to be asked: when we are aware of all this, how does it help us to read the novel? To begin with, to understand the submerged complex of interconnected political and intellectual concerns, ranging from gender to landscape, is to begin to see how Jane Austen's delicate and probing exploration of the psychology of the dependent woman and the social and emotional constraints upon her emerges out of a cluster of problems which were central to her culture. Thus one can begin to see that the novel is a debate about ideas and values negotiated through the characters and happenings at Mansfield Park. The words 'problems' and 'debate' should be emphasized, for one can never map a simple intellectual or political position on to the novel: it is often divided and contradictory about the issues it explores, disclosing their complexity rather than arriving at conclusions. Even the conservative concern with stability and continuity does not unfold as an unproblematic decision in favour of control and resistance to change. On the contrary, the novel recognizes the costs of maintaining a stable world only too sharply.

It is clear that there can be no single view about a novel of such complexity. Since this Critical Study is an introduction, intended to enable students to arrive at a considered exploration of Jane Austen's text, I want to avoid the critic's prescriptive, 'masterly' account of the novel, since this will pre-empt the text and limit the reader's independent thought. So I have attempted to set up the rest of this book as a debate which will put readers in possession of sufficient information and sufficient understanding of the problems of reading a complex text such as this to enable them to arrive at a reading which is as far as possible their own. In the next section of this study, I have assembled a number of writings roughly contemporary with Jane Austen's work which demonstrate some of the intellectual and political concerns I have mentioned above – concerns with religion, education, slavery, women, art and poverty. In order that readers can see for themselves, for instance, what Mrs Inchbald's *Lovers' Vows* is like, I have included some extracts from her play. Readers will have to think about the relevance of these documents to the novel and about the kind of debate the novel is engaging with concerning these topics. The debate emerges in and out of the novel itself, of course, and often involves looking closely at the language and organization of the novel rather than simply assuming that the themes of education or religion, for instance, can be unproblematically transferred from the non-literary text to the fiction.

What I have tried to set up is an exercise in the demands of intertextual reading. After such first-hand acquaintance with some of the issues and problems generated round the reading of *Mansfield Park*, the reader should be ready to enter into a dialogue with the novel and with critical views of the novel. The third section is an essay on *Mansfield Park* which is presented as a reading, but only one reading, which the reader can enter into debate with. The reading is followed by a discussion of the writing of other critics, from Charlotte Brontë to recent writers. The point of this exercise is to show that of all Jane Austen's novels, *Mansfield Park* has raised the most fundamental critical problems. It remains the most problematical novel of her oeuvre. But what these problems are, how they have been interpreted and analysed, has changed from critic to critic and from period to period. A text is not only a single document but that document along with an accretion of interpretation. The excitement of reading *Mansfield Park* is that of understanding that one's own reading is part of this accretion, a new testing-out of interpretation through an exacting and attentive reading of the text.

2. Some Contexts for *Mansfield Park*

The Improper Play, Mrs Inchbald's *Lovers' Vows*

The extract that follows is taken from *Cumberland's British Theatre*, Vol. 17, 1829.

Act II, scene ii

Enter a Servant, L.

Bar. Go directly to Mr Anhalt; tell him I shall be glad to see him for a quarter of an hour if he is not engaged.

[Exit Servant, L.]

Ame. [*Calls after him.*] Wish him a good morning from me.

[Crosses to L.]

Bar. [*Looking at his watch.*] The Count is a tedious time dressing. – Have you breakfasted, Amelia?

Ame. (L.) No, papa.

[*They sit down at table,* L. C. *to breakfast, the Baron,* R. *Amelia,* L.]

Bar. How is the weather? Have you walked this morning?

Ame. Oh, yes – I was in the garden at five o'clock; it is very fine.

Bar. Then I'll go out shooting. I do not know in what other way to amuse my guest.

Enter COUNT CASSEL, R.

Cou. Ah, my dear Colonel! Miss Wildenhaim, I kiss your hand.

Bar. Good morning; good morning! though it is late in the day, count. In the country we should rise earlier.

Cou. [*Crosses to* L.] It is Hebe herself, or Venus, or –

Ame. Ha! ha! ha! Who can help laughing at his nonsense?

Bar. [*Rather angry.*] Neither Venus nor Hebe, but Amelia Wildenhaim, if you please.

[Rises, and goes to the other table, R. C.]

Cou. [*Sitting down to breakfast,* C.] You are beautiful, Miss Wildenhaim. – Upon my honour, I think so. I have travelled, and seen much of the world, and yet I can positively admire you.

Ame. I am sorry I have not seen the world.

Cou. Wherefore? [*Amelia hands the Count a cup of tea.*]

Ame. Because I might then, perhaps, admire you.

Cou. True; – for I am an epitome of the world. In my travels I learnt delicacy in Italy – (a little more cream) – [*Puts his cup over to Amelia*] – hauteur, in Spain – in France, enterprise – in Russia, prudence – in England, sincerity – in Scotland, frugality – (a little more sugar, if you please, Miss Wildenhaim) – in Ireland, hospitality – and in the wilds of America I learnt love.

Ame. Is there any country where love is taught?

Cou. In all barbarous countries. But the whole system is exploded in places that are civilized.

Ame. And what is substituted in its stead?

Cou. Intrigue.

Ame. What a poor uncomfortable substitute!

Cou. There are other things – Song, dance, the opera, and war.

Bar. [*At the table,* R. C.] What are you talking of there?

Cou. Of war, colonel.

Bar. [*Rising.*] Ay, we like to talk on what we don't understand.

Cou. [*Rising.*] Therefore, to a lady, I always speak of politics; and to her father on love.

Bar. [*Comes forward,* R. C.] I believe, count, notwithstanding your sneer, I am still as much of a proficient in that art as yourself.

Cou. [*Comes forward,* C.] I do not doubt it, my dear colonel, for you are a soldier; and, since the days of Alexander, whoever conquers men, is certain to overcome women.

Bar. An achievement to animate a poltroon.

Cou. And, I verily believe, gains more recruits than the king's pay.

Bar. Now we are on the subject of arms, should you like to go out a shooting with me for an hour before dinner?

Cou. Bravo, colonel! A charming thought! This will give me an opportunity to use my elegant gun: the butt is inlaid with mother-of-pearl. You cannot find better work, or better taste. – Even my coat-of-arms is engraved.

Bar. But can you shoot?

Cou. That I have never tried – except with my eyes, at a fine woman.

Bar. I am not particular what game I pursue. – I have an old gun; it does not look fine; but I can always bring down my bird.

Enter SERVANT, L.

Ser. Mr Anhalt begs leave –

Bar. Tell him to come in. – I shall be ready in a moment.

[*Exit Servant,* L.]

Cou. Who is Mr Anhalt?

Ame. [*Rising, coming down,* L.] Oh, a very good man. [*With warmth.*]

Cou. A good man! In Italy, that means a religious man; in France, it means a cheerful man; in Spain, it means a wise man; and in England, it means a rich man. – Which good man of all these is Mr Anhalt?

Ame. A good man in every country except England.

Cou. And give me the English good man before that of any other nation.

Bar. And of what nation would you prefer your good woman to be, count?

Cou. Of Germany.   [*Bowing to Amelia.*]

Ame. In compliment to me?

Cou. In justice to my own judgment.

Bar. Certainly. For have we not an instance of one German woman, who possesses every virtue that ornaments the whole sex; whether as a woman of illustrious rank, or in the more exalted character of a wife and a mother?

Enter MR ANHALT, L. U. E.

Anh. I come by your command, baron –

Bar. Quick, count. Get your elegant gun. I pass your apartments, and will soon call for you.

Cou. I fly – Beautiful Amelia, it is a sacrifice I make to your father, that I leave for a few hours his amiable daughter.   [*Exit,* R.]

Bar. My dear Amelia, I think it scarcely necessary to speak to Mr Anhalt, or that he should speak to you on the subject of the count; but, as he is here, leave us alone.

Ame. [*As she retires.*] Good morning, Mr Anhalt. – I hope you are very well.   [*Exit,* L.]

Bar. (C.) I'll tell you in a few words why I sent for you. Count Cassel is here, and wishes to marry my daughter.

Anh. (L.) [*Much concerned.*] Really!

Bar. He is – he – in a word, I don't like him.

Anh. [*With emotion.*] And Miss Wildenhaim –

Bar. I shall not command, neither persuade her to the marriage – I know too well the fatal influence of parents on such a subject. Objections, to be sure, if they could be removed – but when you find a man's head without brains, and his bosom without a heart, these are important articles to supply. Young as you are, Anhalt, I know no one so able to restore, or to bestow those blessings on his fellow creatures, as you.

[*Anhalt bows.*] The count wants a little of my daughter's simplicity and sensibility. Take him under your care while he is here, and make him something like yourself. You have succeeded to my wish in the education of my daughter. Form the count after your own manner. I shall then have what I have sighed for all my life – a son.

Anh. With your permission, baron, I will presume to ask one question. What remains to interest you in favour of a man whose head and heart are good for nothing?

Bar. Birth and fortune. Yet, if I thought my daughter absolutely disliked him, or that she loved another, I would not thwart a first affection; no, for the world I would not. [*Sighing.*] But that her affections are already bestowed is not probable.

Anh. Are you of opinion that she will never fall in love?

Bar. Oh, no! I am of opinion that no woman ever arrived at the age of twenty without that misfortune – But this is another subject – Go to Amelia, explain to her the duties of a wife, and of a mother – If she comprehends them as she ought, then ask her if she thinks she could fulfil those duties as the wife of Count Cassel.

Anh. I will – But – I – Miss Wildenhaim – [*Confused.*] I – I shall – I – I shall obey your commands.

Bar. Do so. [*Gives a deep sigh.*] Ah! so far this weight is removed; but there lies still a heavier next my heart. You understand me. – How is it, Mr Anhalt? Have you not yet been able to make any discoveries on that unfortunate subject?

Anh. I have taken infinite pains; but in vain. No such person is to be found.

Bar. Believe me, this burden presses on my thoughts so much, that many nights I go without sleep. A man is sometimes tempted to commit such depravity when young – Oh, Anhalt! had I, in my youth, had you for a tutor; but I had no instructor but my passions; no governor but my own will. [*Exit,* L.]

Anh. This commission of the baron's, in respect to his daughter – I am – [*Looks about*]. If I should meet her now, I cannot – I must recover myself first, and then prepare. A walk in the fields, and a fervent prayer. – After these, I trust, I shall return as a man whose views are solely placed on a future world; all hopes in this with fortitude resigned. [*Exit,* I.]

End of Act II.

15

Act III, scene ii

> *A Room in the Castle. – Four chairs.*

Enter AMELIA, L.

Ame. (C.) Why am I so uneasy, so peevish; who has offended me? I did not mean to come into this room. In the garden I intended to go. [*Going*, L. turns back.] No, I will not – yes, I will – just go and look if my auriculas are still in blossom, and if the apple-tree is grown which Mr Anhalt planted. I feel very low-spirited – something must be the matter – Why do I cry? – Am I not well?

Enter MR ANHALT, L.

Ah! good morning, my dear sir – Mr Anhalt, I mean to say. – I beg pardon.

Anh. Never mind, Miss Wildenhaim – I don't dislike to hear you call me as you did.

Ame. In earnest!

Anh. Really. You have been crying. May I know the reason? The loss of your mother, still? –

Ame. No; I have left off crying for her.

Anh. I beg pardon if I have come at an improper hour; but I wait upon you by the commands of your father.

Ame. You are welcome at all hours. My father has more than once told me, that he who forms my mind, I should always consider as my greatest benefactor. [*Looking down.*] And my heart tells me the same.

Anh. I think myself amply rewarded by the good opinion you have of me.

Ame. When I remember what trouble I have sometimes given you, I cannot be too grateful.

Anh. [*To himself.*] Oh, heavens! [*To Amelia.*] I – I come from your father with a commission. – If you please we will sit down. [*He places chairs,* C., *in front, and they sit, Amelia,* R., *Anhalt,* L.] Count Cassel is arrived.

Ame. Yes, I know.

Anh. And do you know for what reason?

Ame. He wishes to marry me.

Anh. Does he? [*Hastily.*] But, believe me, the baron will not persuade you. No, I am sure he will not.

Ame. I know that.

Anh. He wishes that I should ascertain whether you have an inclination –

Ame. For the count, or for matrimony, do you mean?

Anh. For matrimony.

16

Ame. All things that I don't know, and don't understand, are quite indifferent to me.

Anh. For that very reason I am sent to you to explain the good and the bad of which matrimony is composed.

Ame. Then I beg first to be acquainted with the good.

Anh. When two sympathetic hearts meet in the marriage state, matrimony may be called a happy life. When such a wedded pair find thorns in their path, each will be eager, for the sake of the other, to tear them from the root. Where they have to mount hills, or wind a labyrinth, the most experienced will lead the way, and be a guide to his companion. Patience and love will accompany them in their journey, while melancholy and discord they leave far behind. Hand in hand they pass on from morning till evening, through their summer's day, till the night of age draws on, and the sleep of death overtakes the one. The other, weeping and mourning, yet looks forward to the bright region where he shall meet his still surviving partner among trees and flowers, which themselves have planted in the fields of eternal verdure.

Ame. Oh, you may tell my father I'll marry. [*Rising.*]

Anh. [*Rising*] This picture is pleasing; but I must beg you not to forget that there is another on the same subject. When convenience and fair appearance, joined to folly and ill humour, forge the fetters of matrimony, they gall with their weight the married pair. Discontented with each other – at variance in opinions – their mutual aversion increases with the years they live together. They contend most where they should most unite – torment where they should most soothe. In this rugged way, choked with the weeds of suspicion, jealousy, anger, and hatred, they take their daily journey till one of these also sleep in death. The other then lifts up his dejected head, and calls out in acclamations of joy – oh, liberty! dear liberty!

Ame. [*Dejected.*] I will not marry.

Anh. You mean to say you will not fall in love.

Ame. Oh, no! [*Ashamed.*] I am in love.

Anh. Are in love! [*Starting.*] And with the count?

Ame. I wish I was.

Anh. Why so?

Ame. Because he would, perhaps, love me again.

Anh. [*Warmly.*] Who is there that would not?

Ame. Would you?

Anh. I – I – me – I – I am out of the question.

Ame. No; you are the very person to whom I have put the question.

Anh. What do you mean?

17

Ame. I am glad you don't understand me. I was afraid I had spoken too plain. [*Looking down in confusion.*]

Anh. Understand you! As to that – I am not dull.

Ame. I know you are not; and, as you have for a long time instructed me, why should not I now begin to teach you?

Anh. Teach me what?

Ame. Whatever I know and you don't.

Anh. There are some things I had rather never know.

Ame. So, you may remember, I said when you began to teach me mathematics. I said I had rather not know it; but now I have learnt it, it gives me a great deal of pleasure – and [*Hesitating*]. perhaps, who can tell but that I might teach something as pleasant to you as resolving a problem is to me.

Anh. Woman herself is a problem.

Ame. And I'll teach you to make her out.

Anh. You teach?

Ame. Why not? None but a woman can teach the science of herself: and though I own I am very young, a young woman may be as agreeable for a tutoress as an old one. I am sure I always learnt faster from you than from the old clergyman who taught me before you came.

Anh. This is nothing to the subject.

Ame. What is the subject?

Anh. Love.

Ame. [*Going up to him.*] Come, then, teach it me – teach it me as you taught me geography, languages, and other important things.

Anh. [*Turning from her.*] Pshaw!

Ame. Ah! you won't – you know you have already taught me that, and you won't begin again.

Anh. You misconstrue – you misconceive every thing I say or do. The subject I came to you upon was marriage.

Ame. A very proper subject for the man who has taught me love, and I accept the proposal. [*Curtsying.*]

Anh. Again you misconceive and confound me.

Ame. Ay, I see how it is, – you have no inclination to experience with me "the good part of matrimony:" I am not the female with whom you would like to go "hand in hand up hills, and through labyrinths" – with whom you would like to "root up thorns; and with whom you would delight to plant lilies and roses." No; you had rather call out, – "Oh, liberty! dear liberty!"

Anh. Why do you force from me what it is villainous to own? – I love you more than life. Oh, Amelia! had we lived in those golden times which the poets picture, no one but you – But, as the world is changed, your birth and fortune make – Our union is impossible – To preserve the character, and, more, the feelings of an honest man, I would not marry you without the consent of your father; and could I, dare I, propose it to him?

Ame. He has commanded me never to conceal or disguise the truth. I will propose it to him. The subject of the count will force me to speak plainly, and this will be the most proper time, while he can compare the merit of you both.

Anh. I conjure you not to think of exposing yourself and me to his resentment.

Ame. It is my father's will that I should marry – it is my father's wish to see me happy. – If, then, you love me as you say, I will marry, and will be happy – but only with you. I will tell him this. At first he will start – then grow angry – then be in a passion. In his passion he will call me "undutiful:" but he will soon recollect himself, and resume his usual smiles, saying, "Well, well, if he love you, and you love him, in the name of heaven, let it be." – Then I shall hug him round the neck, kiss his hands, run away from him, and fly to you; it will soon be known that I am your bride, the whole village will come to wish me joy, and heaven's blessing will follow.

Landscape Gardening, Sir Humphrey Repton

The extract that follows is taken from Sir Humphrey Repton's *An Enquiry into the Changes of Taste in Landscape Gardening*, 1806, though the first two paragraphs were first written in 1794.

It seems to have been as much the fashion of the present century to destroy avenues, as it was in the last to plant them; and while many people think they sufficiently justify their opinion, in either case, by saying, 'I like an avenue', or 'I hate an avenue', let us endeavour to analyse this approbation or disgust.

The pleasure which the mind derives from the love of *Order*, of *Unity*, of *Antiquity*, and of *Continuity*, are in a certain degree gratified by the long perspective view of a stately avenue; even when it consists of trees in rows so far apart, that their branches do not touch: but where they grow so near as to imitate the grandeur, the gloomy shade, and almost the shelter of a Gothic cathedral, we may add the *Comfort* and *Convenience* of such an avenue to all the other considerations of its beauty. A long avenue, terminated by a large old mansion, is a magnificent object, although it may not be a proper subject for a picture; but the view from such a mansion is perhaps among the greatest objections to an avenue, because it destroys all variety . . . But the greatest objection to an avenue is, that (especially in uneven ground) it often acts as a curtain drawn across the most interesting scenery: it is in undrawing this curtain at proper places that the utility of what has been called breaking an avenue consists . . . but the change of fashion in Gardening destroys the work of ages, when lofty avenues are cut down for no other reason but because they were planted in straight lines.

Appropriation. A word . . . lately coined by me, to describe extent of property . . . a source of pleasure not to be disregarded; since every individual who possesses anything, whether it be mental endowments, or power, or property, obtains respect in proportion as his possessions are known, provided he does not too vainly boast of them . . . The pleasure of appropriation is gratified in viewing a landscape which cannot be injured by the malice or bad taste of a neighbouring intruder: thus an ugly barn, a ploughed field, or any intrusive object which disgraces the scenery of a park, looks as if it belonged to another, and therefore robs the mind of the pleasure derived from appropriation, or the unity and continuity of unmixed property.

Femininity, Mary Wollstonecraft

The extract that follows is taken from Mary Wollstonecraft's *Vindication of the Rights of Woman*, 1792.

CHAPTER 2

The Prevailing Opinion of a Sexual
Character Discussed

To account for, and excuse the tyranny of man, many ingenious arguments have been brought forward to prove, that the two sexes, in the acquirement of virtue, ought to aim at attaining a very different character; or, to speak explicitly, women are not allowed to have sufficient strength of mind to acquire what really deserves the name of virtue. Yet it should seem, allowing them to have souls, that there is but one way appointed by Providence to lead *mankind* to either virtue or happiness.

If then women are not a swarm of ephemeron triflers, why should they be kept in ignorance under the specious name of innocence? Men complain, and with reason, of the follies and caprices of our sex, when they do not keenly satirise our headstrong passions and grovelling vices. Behold, I should answer, the natural effect of ignorance! The mind will ever be unstable that has only prejudices to rest on, and the current will run with destructive fury when there are no barriers to break its force. Women are told from their infancy, and taught by the example of their mothers, that a little knowledge of human weakness, justly termed cunning, softness of temper, *outward* obedience, and a scrupulous attention to a puerile kind of propriety, will obtain for them the protection of man; and should they be beautiful, everything else is needless, for at least twenty years of their lives.

Thus Milton describes our first frail mother; though when he tells us that women are formed for softness and sweet attractive grace, I cannot comprehend his meaning, unless, in the true Mahometan strain, he meant to deprive us of souls, and insinuate that we were beings only designed by sweet attractive grace, and docile blind obedience, to gratify the senses of man when he can no longer soar on the wing of contemplation.

How grossly do they insult us who thus advise us only to render ourselves gentle, domestic brutes! For instance, the winning softness so warmly and frequently recommended, that governs by obeying. What childish expressions, and how insignificant is the being – can it be an immortal one? – who will condescend to govern by such sinister methods? 'Certainly,' says Lord Bacon, 'man is of kin to the beasts by his body; and if he be not of kin to God by his spirit, he is a base and ignoble creature!' Men, indeed, appear to me to act in a very unphilosophical manner, when they try to secure the good conduct of women by attempting to keep them always in a state of childhood. Rousseau was more consistent when he wished to stop the progress of reason in both sexes, for if men eat of the tree of knowledge, women will come in for a taste; but, from the imperfect cultivation which their understandings now receive, they only attain a knowledge of evil.

Children, I grant, should be innocent; but when the epithet is applied to men, or women, it is but a civil term for weakness. For if it be allowed that women were destined by Providence to acquire human virtues, and, by the exercise of their understandings, that stability of character which is the firmest ground to rest our future hopes upon, they must be permitted to turn to the fountain of light, and not forced to shape their course by the twinkling of a mere satellite. Milton, I grant, was of a very different opinion; for he only bends to the indefeasible right of beauty, though it would be difficult to render two passages which I now mean to contrast, consistent. But into similar inconsistencies are great men often led by their senses:

> To whom thus Eve with *perfect beauty* adorn'd.
> My author and disposer, what thou bid'st
> *Unargued* I obey; so God ordains;
> God is *thy law, thou mine*: to know no more
> Is woman's *happiest* knowledge and her *praise*.

... Consequently, the most perfect education, in my opinion, is such an exercise of the understanding as is best calculated to strengthen the body and form the heart. Or, in other words, to enable the individual to attain such habits of virtue as will render it independent. In fact, it is a farce to call any being virtuous whose virtues do not result from the exercise of its own reason. This was Rousseau's opinion respecting men; I extend it to women, and confidently assert that they have been drawn out of their sphere by false refinement, and not by an endeavour to acquire masculine qualities. Still the regal homage which they receive is so intoxicating, that until the manners of the times are changed, and formed on more reasonable principles, it may be impossible to convince them that the illegitimate power which they obtain by degrading themselves is a curse, and that they must return to nature and equality if they wish to secure the placid satisfaction that unsophisticated affections impart. But for this epoch we must wait – wait perhaps till kings and nobles, enlightened by reason, and, preferring the real dignity of man to childish state, throw off their gaudy hereditary trappings; and if then women do not resign the arbitrary power of beauty – they will prove that they have *less* mind than man ...

Standing armies can never consist of resolute robust men; they may be well-disciplined machines, but they will seldom contain men under the influence of strong passions, or with very vigorous faculties; and as for any depth of understanding, I will venture to affirm that it is as rarely to be found in the army as amongst women. And the cause, I maintain, is the same. It may be further observed that officers are also particularly attentive to their persons, fond of dancing, crowded rooms, adventures, and ridicule.[1] Like the *fair* sex, the business of their lives is gallantry;

1 Why should women be censured with petulant acrimony because they seem to have a passion for a scarlet coat? Has not education placed them more on a level with soldiers than any other class of men?

they were taught to please, and they only live to please. Yet they do not lose their rank in the distinction of sexes, for they are still reckoned superior to women, though in what their superiority consists, beyond what I have just mentioned, it is difficult to discover.

The great misfortune is this, that they both acquire manners before morals, and a knowledge of life before they have from reflection any acquaintance with the grand ideal outline of human nature. The consequence is natural. Satisfied with common nature, they become a prey to prejudices, and taking all their opinions on credit, they blindly submit to authority. So that if they have any sense, it is a kind of instinctive glance that catches proportions, and decides with respect to manners, but fails when arguments are to be pursued below the surface, or opinions analysed.

May not the same remark be applied to women? Nay, the argument may be carried still further, for they are both thrown out of a useful station by the unnatural distinctions established in civilized life. Riches and hereditary honours have made cyphers of women to give consequence to the numerical figure; and idleness has produced a mixture of gallantry and despotism into society, which leads the very men who are the slaves of their mistresses to tyrannize over their sisters, wives, and daughters. This is only keeping them in rank and file, it is true. Strengthen the female mind by enlarging it, and there will be an end to blind obedience; but as blind obedience is ever sought for by power, tyrants and sensualists are in the right when they endeavour to keep woman in the dark, because the former only want slaves, and the latter a plaything. The sensualist, indeed, has been the most dangerous of tyrants, and women have been duped by their lovers, as princes by their ministers, whilst dreaming that they reigned over them . . .

Of the same complexion is Dr Gregory's advice respecting delicacy of sentiment, which he advises a woman not to acquire, if she have determined to marry. This determination, however, perfectly consistent with his former advice, he calls *indelicate*, and earnestly persuades his daughters to conceal it, though it may govern their conduct, as if it were indelicate to have the common appetites of human nature . . .

Gentleness of manners, forbearance and long suffering, are such amiable Godlike qualities, that in sublime poetic strains the Deity has been invested with them; and, perhaps, no representation of His goodness so strongly fastens on the human affections as those that represent Him abundant in mercy and willing to pardon. Gentleness, considered in this point of view, bears on its front all the characteristics of grandeur, combined with the winning graces of condescension; but what a different aspect it assumes when it is the submissive demeanour of dependence, the support of weakness that loves, because it wants protection; and is forbearing, because it must silently endure injuries; smiling under the lash at which it dare not snarl. Abject as this picture appears, it is the portrait of an accomplished woman, according to the received opinion of female excellence, separated by specious reasoners from human excellence . . .

CHAPTER 3

The Same Subject Continued

. . . I once knew a weak woman of fashion, who was more than commonly proud of her delicacy and sensibility. She thought a distinguishing taste and puny appetite the height of all human perfection, and acted accordingly. I have seen this weak sophisticated being neglect all the duties of life, yet recline with self-complacency on a sofa, and boast of her want of appetite as a proof of delicacy that extended to, or, perhaps, arose from, her exquisite sensibility; for it is difficult to render intelligible such ridiculous jargon.

Education, John Locke and William Wordsworth

The first extract is taken from John Locke's *On Education*, 1693, published in *Works*, Vol. IX, 1823 (reprinted 1963).

Governor.

90 In all the whole business of education, there is nothing like to be less hearkened to, or harder to be well observed, than what I am now going to say; and that is, that children should, from their first beginning to talk, have some discreet, sober, nay wise person about them, whose care it should be to fashion them aright, and keep them from all ill, especially the infection of bad company. I think this province requires great sobriety, temperance, tenderness, diligence, and discretion; qualities hardly

to be found united in persons that are to be had for ordinary salaries, nor easily to be found anywhere. As to the charge of it, I think it will be the money best laid out that can be about our children; and therefore, though it may be expensive more than is ordinary, yet it cannot be thought dear. He that at any rate procures his child a good mind, well-principled, tempered to virtue and usefulness, and adorned with civility and good breeding, makes a better purchase for him, than if he had laid out the money for an addition of more earth to his former acres. Spare it in toys and play-games, in silk and ribbons, laces and other useless expenses, as much as you please; but be not sparing in so necessary a part as this. It is not good husbandry to make his fortune rich, and his mind poor. I have often, with great admiration, seen people lavish it profusely in tricking up their children in fine clothes, lodging, and feeding them sumptuously, allowing them more than enough of useless servants; and yet at the same time starve their minds, and not take sufficient care to cover that which is the most shameful nakedness, viz. their natural wrong inclinations and ignorance . . .

Familiarity.

95 But to return to our method again. Though I have mentioned the severity of the father's brow, and the awe settled thereby in the mind of children when young, as one main instrument, whereby their education is to be managed; yet I am far from being of an opinion, that it should be continued all along to them: whilst they are under the discipline and government of pupilage, I think it should be relaxed, as fast as their age, discretion, and good behaviour could allow it; even to that degree, that a father will do well, as his son grows up, and is capable of it, to talk familiarly with him; nay, ask his advice, and consult with him, about those things wherein he has any knowledge or understanding. By this the father will gain two things, both of great moment. The one is, that it will put serious considerations into his son's thoughts, better than any rules or advices he can give him. The sooner you treat him as a man, the sooner he will begin to be one: and if you admit him into serious discourses sometimes with you, you will insensibly raise his mind above the usual amusements of youth, and those trifling occupations which it is commonly wasted in. For it is easy to observe, that many young men continue longer in the thought and conversation of schoolboys, than otherwise they would, because their parents keep them at that distance, and in that low rank, by all their carriage to them.

96 Another thing of greater consequence, which you will obtain by

such a way of treating him, will be his friendship. Many fathers, though they proportion to their sons liberal allowances, according to their age and condition; yet they keep the knowledge of their estates and concerns from them with as much reservedness as if they were guarding a secret of state from a spy or an enemy. This, if it looks not like jealousy, yet it wants those marks of kindness and intimacy, which a father should show to his son; and, no doubt, often hinders or abates that cheerfulness and satisfaction, wherewith a son should address himself to, and rely upon, his father. And I cannot but often wonder to see fathers, who love their sons very well, yet so order the matter, by a constant stiffness, and a mien of authority and distance to them all their lives, as if they were never to enjoy or have any comfort from those they love best in the world till they have lost them by being removed into another. Nothing cements and establishes friendship and good-will so much as confident communication of concernments and affairs. Other kindnesses, without this, leave still some doubts; but when your son sees you open your mind to him; when he finds that you interest him in your affairs, as things you are willing should, in their turn, come into his hands, he will be concerned for them as for his own; wait his season with patience, and love you in the mean time, who keep him not at the distance of a stranger. This will also make him see, that the enjoyment you have, is not without care; which the more he is sensible of, the less will he envy you the possession, and the more think himself happy under the management of so favourable a friend, and so careful a father . . .

97 But whatever he consults you about, unless it lead to some fatal and irremediable mischief, be sure you advise only as a friend of more experience; but with your advice mingle nothing of command or authority, nor more than you would to your equal, or a stranger. That would be to drive him for ever from any farther demanding, or receiving advantage from your counsel. You must consider, that he is a young man, and has pleasures and fancies, which you are passed. You must not expect his inclinations should be just as yours, nor that at twenty he should have the same thoughts you have at fifty. All that you can wish is, that since youth must have some liberty, some out-leaps; they might be with the ingenuity of a son, and under the eye of a father, and then no very great harm can come of it. The way to obtain this, as I said before, is (according as you find him capable) to talk with him about your affairs, propose matters to him familiarly, and ask his advice; and when he ever lights on the right, follow it as his; and if it succeed well, let him have the commendation. This will not at all lessen your authority, but increase his love and esteem of you. Whilst you keep your estate, the staff will still be

in your own hands; and your authority the surer, the more it is strengthened with confidence and kindness. For you have not that power you ought to have over him, till he comes to be more afraid of offending so good a friend than of losing some part of his future expectation.

98 Familiarity of discourse, if it can become a father to his son, may much more be condescended to by a tutor to his pupil. All their time together should not be spent in reading of lectures, and magisterially dictating to him what he is to observe and follow; hearing him in his turn, and using him to reason about what is proposed, will make the rules go down the easier, and sink the deeper, and will give him a liking to study and instruction: and he will then begin to value knowledge, when he sees that it enables him to discourse; and he finds the pleasure and credit of bearing a part in the conversation, and of having his reasons sometimes approved and hearkened to. Particularly in morality, prudence, and breeding, cases should be put to him, and his judgment asked: this opens the understanding better than maxims, how well soever explained; and settles the rules better in the memory for practice. This way lets things into the mind, which stick there, and retain their evidence with them; whereas words at best are faint representations, being not so much as the true shadows of things, and are much sooner forgotten. He will better comprehend the foundations and measures of decency and justice, and have livelier and more lasting impressions of what he ought to do, by giving his opinion on cases proposed, and reasoning with his tutor on fit instances, than by giving a silent, negligent, sleepy audience to his tutor's lectures . . .

176 I hear it is said, that children should be employed in getting things by heart, to exercise and improve their memories. I could wish this were said with as much authority of reason, as it is with forwardness of assurance; and that this practice were established upon good observation, more than old custom; for it is evident, that strength of memory is owing to a happy constitution, and not to any habitual improvement got by exercise. It is true, what the mind is intent upon, and for fear of letting it slip, often imprints afresh on itself by frequent reflection, that it is apt to retain, but still according to its own natural strength of retention. An impression made on bees-wax or lead will not last so long as on brass or steel. Indeed, if it be renewed often, it may last the longer; but every new reflecting on it is a new impression, and it is from thence one is to reckon, if one would know how long the mind retains it. But the learning pages of Latin by heart, no more fits the memory for retention of any thing else, than the graving of one sentence in lead, makes it the more capable of retaining firmly any other characters. If such a sort of exercise

27

of the memory were able to give it strength, and improve our parts, players of all other people must needs have the best memories, and be the best company: but whether the scraps they have got into their head this way, make them remember other things the better; and whether their parts be improved proportionably to the pains they have taken in getting by heart other sayings; experience will show. Memory is so necessary to all parts and conditions of life, and so little is to be done without it, that we are not to fear it should grow dull and useless for want of exercise, if exercise would make it grow stronger . . .

178 Geography, I think, should be begun with; for the learning of the figure of the globe, the situation and boundaries of the four parts of the world, and that of particular kingdoms and countries, being only an exercise of the eyes and memory, a child with pleasure will learn and retain them: and this is so certain, that I now live in the house with a child, whom his mother has so well instructed this way in geography, that he knew the limits of the four parts of the world, could readily point, being asked, to any country upon the globe, or any county in the map of England; knew all the great rivers, promontories, straits, and bays in the world, and could find the longitude and latitude of any place, before he was six years old. These things, that he will thus learn by sight, and have by rote in his memory, are not all, I confess, that he is to learn upon the globes. But yet it is a good step and preparation to it, and will make the remainder much easier, when his judgment is grown ripe enough for it: besides that, it gets so much time now, and by the pleasure of knowing things, leads him on insensibly to the gaining of languages.

The second extract is taken from William Wordsworth's *The Prelude*, Book V, lines 290–69, 1805.

> My drift hath scarcely
> I fear been obvious, for I have recoiled
> From showing as it is the monster birth
> Engendered by these too industrious times.
> Let few words paint it: 'tis a child, no child,
> But a dwarf man; in knowledge, virtue, skill,
> In what he is not, and in what he is,
> The noontide shadow of a man complete;
> A worshipper of worldly seemliness –
> Not quarrelsome, for that were far beneath
> His dignity; with gifts he bubbles o'er
> As generous as a fountain; selfishness
> May not come near him, gluttony or pride;

The wandering beggars propagate his name,
Dumb creatures find him tender as a nun.
Yet deem him not for this a naked dish
Of goodness merely – he is garnished out.
Arch are his notices, and nice his sense
Of the ridiculous; deceit and guile,
Meanness and falsehood, he detects, can treat
With apt and graceful laughter; nor is blind
To the broad follies of the licensed world;
Though shrewd, yet innocent himself withal,
And can read lectures upon innocence.
He is fenced round, nay armed, for ought we know,
In panoply complete; and fear itself,
Natural or supernatural alike,
Unless it leap upon him in a dream,
Touches him not. Briefly, the moral part
Is perfect, and in learning and in books
He is a prodigy. His discourse moves slow,
Massy and ponderous as a prison door,
Tremendously embossed with terms of art.
Rank growth of propositions overruns
The stripling's brain; the path in which he treads
Is choked with grammars. Cushion of divine
Was never such a type of thought profound
As is the pillow where he rests his head.
The ensigns of the empire which he holds –
The globe and sceptre of his royalties –
Are telescopes, and crucibles, and maps.
Ships he can guide across the pathless sea,
And tell you all their cunning; he can read
The inside of the earth, and spell the stars;
He knows the policies of foreign lands,
Can string you names of districts, cities, towns,
The whole world over, tight as beads of dew
Upon a gossamer thread. He sifts, he weighs,
Takes nothing upon trust. His teachers stare,
The country people pray for God's good grace,
And tremble at his deep experiments.
All things are put to question: he must live
Knowing that he grows wiser every day,
Or else not live at all, and seeing too
Each little drop of wisdom as it falls
Into the dimpling cistern of his heart.
Meanwhile old Grandame Earth is grieved to find
The playthings which her love designed for him

Unthought of – in their woodland beds the flowers
Weep, and the river-sides are all forlorn.

Now this is hollow, 'tis a life of lies
From the beginning, and in lies must end.
Forth bring him to the air of common sense
And, fresh and shewy as it is, the corps
Slips from us into powder. Vanity,
That is his soul: there lives he, and there moves –
It is the soul of every thing he seeks –
That gone, nothing is left which he can love.
Nay, if a thought of purer birth should rise
To carry him towards a better clime,
Some busy helper still is on the watch
To drive him back, and pound him like a stray
With the pinfold of his own conceit,
Which is his home, his natural dwelling-place.
Oh, give us once again the wishing-cap
Of Fortunatus, and the invisible coat
Of Jack the Giant-killer, Robin Hood,
And Sabra in the forest with St George!
The child whose love is here, at least doth reap
One precious gain – that he forgets himself.

The French Revolution, Property and Representative Government, Edmund Burke

The extract that follows is taken from Edmund Burke's *Reflections on the Revolution in France*, 1790, published in *Works*, Vol. V, 1826.

The power of perpetuating our property in our families is one of the most valuable and interesting circumstances belonging to it, and that which tends the most to the perpetuation of society itself. It makes our weakness subservient to our virtue; it grafts benevolence even upon avarice. The possessors of family wealth, and of the distinction which attends hereditary possession, (as most concerned in it) are the natural securities for this transmission. With us the house of peers is formed upon this principle. It is wholly composed of hereditary property and hereditary distinction; and made therefore the third of the legislature; and, in the last event, the sole judge of all property in all its subdivisions. The house of commons too, though not necessarily, yet in fact, is always so composed, in the far greater part. Let those large proprietors be what they will, and they have their chance of being among the best, they are, at the very worst, the ballast in the vessel of the commonwealth. For though hereditary wealth, and the rank which goes with it, are too much idolized by creeping sycophants, and the blind, abject admirers of power, they are too rashly slighted in shallow speculations of the petulant, assuming, short-sighted coxcombs of philosophy. Some decent, regulated pre-eminence, some preference (not exclusive appropriation) given to birth, is neither unnatural, nor unjust, nor impolitick.

It is said, that twenty-four millions ought to prevail over two hundred thousand. True; if the constitution of a kingdom be a problem of arithmetick. This sort of discourse does well enough with the lamp-post for its second: to men who *may* reason calmly, it is ridiculous. The will of the many, and their interest, must very often differ; and great will be the difference when they make an evil choice. A government of five hundred country attornies and obscure curates is not good for twenty-four millions of men, though it were chosen by eight and forty millions . . .

I see that your example is held out to shame us. I know that we are supposed a dull, sluggish race, rendered passive by finding our situation tolerable, and prevented by a mediocrity of freedom from ever attaining to its full perfection. Your leaders in France began by affecting to admire, almost to adore, the British constitution; but, as they advanced, they came to look upon it with a sovereign contempt. The friends of your National Assembly amongst us have full as mean an opinion of what was formerly thought the glory of their country. The Revolution Society has discovered that the English nation is not free. They are convinced that the inequality in our representation is a 'defect in our constitution *so gross and palpable*, as to make it excellent chiefly in *form* and *theory*.' That a representation in the legislature of a kingdom is not only the basis of all constitutional liberty in it, but of '*all legitimate government*; that without it a *government* is nothing but an *usurpation*;' – that 'when the representation is *partial*, the kingdom possesses liberty only *partially*; and if extremely partial, it gives only a *semblance*; and if not only extremely partial, but corruptly chosen, it becomes a *nuisance*.' . . .

A cheap, bloodless reformation, a guiltless liberty, appear flat and vapid to their taste. There must be a great change of scene; there must be a magnificent stage effect; there must be a grand spectacle to rouse the imagination, grown torpid with the lazy enjoyment of sixty years security, and the still unanimating repose of publick prosperity. The preacher found them all in the French Revolution. This inspires a juvenile warmth through his whole frame . . .

But now all is to be changed. All the pleasing illusions, which made power gentle, and obedience liberal, which harmonized the different shades of life, and which, by a bland assimilation, incorporated into politicks the sentiments which beautify and soften private society, are to be dissolved by this new conquering empire of light and reason. All the decent drapery of life is to be rudely torn off. All the superadded ideas, furnished from the wardrobe of a moral imagination, which the heart owns, and the understanding ratifies, as necessary to cover the defects of our naked, shivering nature, and to raise it to dignity in our own estimation, are to be exploded as a ridiculous, absurd, and antiquated fashion.

On this scheme of things, a king is but a man, a queen is but a woman; a woman is but an animal; and an animal not of the highest order . . .

Indeed the theatre is a better school of moral sentiments than churches, where the feelings of humanity are thus outraged. Poets who have to deal with an audience not yet graduated in the school of the rights of men, and who must apply themselves to the moral constitution of the heart, would not dare to produce such a triumph as a matter of exultation. There, where men follow their natural impulses, they would not bear the odius maxims of a Machiavellian policy, whether applied to the attainment of monarchical or democratick tyranny. They would reject them on the modern, as they once did on the ancient stage, where they could not bear even the hypothetical proposition of such wickedness in the mouth of a personated tyrant, though suitable to the character he sustained. No theatrick audience in Athens would bear what has been borne, in the midst of the real tragedy of this triumphal day; a principal actor weighing, as it were in scales hung in a shop of horrours, – so much actual crime against so much contingent advantage, – and after putting in and out weights, declaring that the balance was on the side of the advantages. They would not bear to see the crimes of new democracy posted as in a ledger against the crimes of old despotism, and the book-keepers of politicks finding democracy still in debt, but by no means unable or unwilling to pay the balance. In the theatre, the first intuitive glance, without any elaborate process of reasoning, will shew, that this method of political computation would justify every extent of crime. They would see, that on these principles, even where the very worst acts were not perpetrated, it was owing rather to the fortune of the conspirators, than to their parsimony in the expenditure of treachery and blood. They would soon see, that criminal means once tolerated are soon preferred . . .

It is on some such principles that the majority of the people of England, far from thinking a religious national establishment unlawful, hardly think it lawful to be without one. In France you are wholly mistaken if you do not believe us above all other things attached to it, and beyond all other nations; and when this people has acted unwisely and unjustifiably in its favour (as in some instances they have done most certainly) in their very errours you will at least discover their zeal.

This principle runs through the whole system of their polity. They do not consider their church establishment as convenient, but as essential to their state; not as a thing heterogeneous and separable; something added for accommodation; what they may either keep or lay aside, according to their temporary ideas of convenience. They consider it as the foundation of their whole constitution, with which, and with every part of which, it holds an indissoluble union. Church and state are ideas inseparable in their minds, and scarcely is the one ever mentioned without mentioning the other.

The Wars in France and the Condition of the Poor, Robert Southey

The first extract is taken from Robert Southey's 'On Parliamentary Reform; On the Conduct of the War', 1810, published in *Essays Moral and Political*, 1832.

The constitution is an excellent war-cry for a party . . . 'Nothing but the Constitution!' . . . But what do they, who use this cry, mean by the Constitution which they call for? For there is not a greater difference between the same individual, in the days of his childhood, of his youth, manhood, maturity, and old age, than in the system of the English government at different periods of its history.

The fact is, that the Constitution is *not* to be found in the Statute Book: . . . we have no nine-and-thirty articles of state. The history of our government is like that of our common law. A system has grown up among us unlike that of our ancestors, or of any other people; and that system, such as it is, has made us the prosperous, the powerful, the free, . . . would that it might be added . . . the *happy* people that we are! Better systems, no doubt, are conceivable . . . for better men. The theory of a pure republic is far more delightful to the imagination: it is to our constitution as a sun-dial to a time-piece, simpler, surer, and liable to no derangement . . . if the sun did but always shine . . .

They who propose oaths for the elected, that no money or influence has been used in obtaining their election, should invent an oath also that there has been none of this fouler corruption . . . no making the people drunk with sedition, . . . no bribing them with lying promises: for this would be the currency if all elections were made popular, and the influence of wealth and power destroyed. It is easy to see who would be the successful candidates at such elections: ... not men whose names and families are older in the country than the old oaks upon their estates, and who possess the habitual and hereditary respect and confidence of all around them; ... not they who have made their own fortunes, and, with an honourable ambition, are desirous of serving and supporting, as best they can, the country and the government in which and under which they have prospered; ... not the soldier and the sailor, who, having upheld the honour of England abroad, would fain in the evening of life sustain her interests at home; ... not the lawyer who is at the head of his profession; ... not the man of learning, the financier, the statesman, and the philosopher: ... but hotheaded and presumptuous youth; the old, to whom years have brought no knowledge; the adventurer; the gambler, who would sport with the fortunes of his country as lightly as he sets his own upon the die; the unsuccessful, the disappointed, and the desperate. These would be the successful candidates; these would be the popular leaders ...

If any real reform in the representation be practicable, it is either by electing the electors, and thus filtering them through successive processes, after the manner of the Spanish Cortes; – (and for a pure legislative body, in which there is no party embodied against the government, this mode is unexceptionable:) or, it might be better effected among us by raising the value of a freehold to what it originally was, and thus taking away votes from the ignorant, who cannot possibly know how to use them. A man ought well to have studied history before he is fit for any direct share in national policy; and certainly his constituents should be within reach of reading history if they please. All the errors which prevailed in this country respecting the French revolution proceeded from ignorance: no man who was acquainted with the history of the *Fronde* could have expected any happy result from a revolution in France, the French being what they were; no man who had studied Machiavelli could have committed the blunders which were committed in the conduct of the anti-jacobin war. But wealth of some kind, by whatever legal criterion to be indicated, is necessary to education and sound thought on policy, ... a science which, of all others, tempts men to think it easy, while it is in reality the most difficult of all.

The real evil of our representation lies, not in the influence of the Treasury, but in the power of a few great land-holders, ... in that power which enables one of these political behemoths to demand for himself an office, or at least to exercise an influence in the government, though he should have no pretensions to it on the score of abilities or character. This is a power which no oath can reach, and which Mr Curwen's bill renders more monstrous, by destroying, or attempting to destroy, all that counterbalanced it. An evil it is, and a great evil; but it is one which the increasing wealth of the country must continually diminish . . .

The main evil of our government is not in the state of the representation, but in the want of an efficient head. In time of war, a cabinet, like an aulic council, seems to insure vacillation and imbecility: it proceeds by a system of concessions and compromises, which renders it incapable of anything vigorous or decisive. We want a responsible prime minister, to whom all the departments of state should be subordinate . . .

For him who has the business of true reform, that is, who has the desire of benefiting his country and his kind, sincerely at heart, there is work enough in the world, be his temper and the nature of his talents what they may. Benevolence, however active, may find sufficient employment in those plans, so peculiarly honourable to England, which are at this time carrying on for bettering the condition of the poor, for preventing poverty and guilt by national education, for sowing the seeds of civilization in Africa, and for extending the blessings of Christianity to the degraded nations of the East, the brutalized tribes of Polynesia, the Tartar hordes, the Negroes, and the poor Hottentots, . . . now subjects of our own government, the most inoffensive of men, and hitherto the most wickedly oppressed. If his ambition be to figure in Parliament as a political reformer, there also good is to be done, in which, let but practicable plans be brought forward, any ministry will be most ready to co-operate: the poor laws and the penal laws require revision, and means are still desired for preventing the necessity of pressing for the navy. Is it difficult to amend one of these things? oh then be sure it is far more so to amend the system which includes them all! . . . Should it be his humour to ferret out abuses? Let him look to the contractors, . . . those, for instance, whose biscuit is known in the navy by the name of 'composition-cake,' over which their malediction is piously drank as a standing toast in the ward-room. Or let him examine into the state of the charitable foundations over the country, where the same number of poor persons are now maintained in the same manner as when the institutions were endowed centuries ago; and the increase of the rent, which in some places is twenty, fifty, even an hundred fold, is swallowed up by chaplains and trustees. But if he be indeed a patriot, in the genuine sense of that polluted name, . . . if he has in him a deep, and dutiful, and enlightened love of the country in which it has been his happy privilege to be born, . . . he will feel that in these times the paramount duty of an

Englishman is, to exert himself in raising the spirit of his countrymen to the pitch of those days, when they won crowns and brought home captive kings. The one business of England is to abate the power of France; that power she must beat down, or fall herself; that power she will beat down, if she do but wisely and strenuously put forth her own mighty means.

A nation engaging in war without a deep conviction of the necessity of obtaining its object, must act more by chance than by foresight; difficulties which have not been foreseen are, when they arise, magnified into impossibilities; and they occasion either the sudden abandonment of an enterprize lightly begun, or such a vacillation both in the cabinet and the field, that the opportunities of action are lost, and success becomes impossible. These few words comprise the history of all our military failures. A general want of information has always been complained of by the British army; countries have been found quite different from the notions entertained of them; the maps and plans in our possession have proved erroneous, and the disposition of the natives has disappointed our expectations. Now, information upon all these points is certainly and easily to be obtained, . . . but not on the spur of the moment; it must be the work of foresight, and would not have been neglected, had the nation felt more strongly the importance of its wars by land. A more unaccountable, and far more mischievous cause of failure is, that in almost all our military expeditions, the force employed has been inadequate to the object proposed. It is no economy, says Captain Pasley, either of money or of lives, to make war by driblets. We ought to deal in war by wholesale; fifties of thousands bring home princely returns to the enterprising merchant; the gains of the timid trader, even when he gains, are little in proportion to the little that he has risked upon the adventure; and by cautiously shifting his capital from one branch of commerce to another he sees bolder competitors outstrip him in all, and perhaps ruins himself at last from a fear of bankruptcy.

The second extract is taken from Robert Southey's 'On the State of the Poor', 1812.

The improved system of farming has lessened the comforts of the poor. It has either deprived the cottager of those slips of land which contributed greatly to his support, or it has placed upon them an excessive and grinding rent. But as the comforts of the cottager are diminished, his respectability and his self-respect are diminished also, and hence arises a long train of evils. The practice of farming upon a great scale has unquestionably improved the agriculture of the country; better crops are raised at less expense: but in a national point of view, there is something more to be considered than the produce of the land and the profit of the landholders. The well-being of the people is not of less importance than the wealth of the collective body. By the system of adding field to field, more has been lost to the state than has been gained to the soil: the gain may be measured by roods and perches, . . . but how shall the loss be calculated? The loss is that of a link in the social chain, . . . of a numerous, most useful, and most respectable class, who, from the rank of small farmers, have been degraded to that of day-labourers. True it is, that the ground which they occupied is more highly cultivated . . . the crooked hedge-rows have been thrown down . . . the fields are in better shape and of handsomer dimensions . . . the plough makes longer furrows . . . there is more corn and fewer weeds; . . . but look at the noblest produce of the earth . . . look at the children of the soil . . . look at the seeds which are sown here for immortality! Is there no deterioration there? Does the man stand upon the same level in society, . . . does he hold the same place in his own estimation, when he works for another as when he works for himself; when he receives his daily wages for the sweat of his brow, and there the fruit of his labour ends, as when he enjoys day by day the advantage of his former toil, and works always in hope of the recompense which is always to come? The small farmer, or, in the language of Latimer and old English feeling, the yeoman, had his roots in the soil: . . . this was the right English tree in which our heart of oak was matured. Where he grew up, he decayed: where he first opened his eyes, there he fell asleep . . .

While the spirit of jacobinism had thus evaporated from the top of the vessel, its dregs were settling at the bottom. It had lost its generalizing spirit and its metaphysics: whatever, also, had made it alluring to the young, and ardent, and enthusiastic lovers of their kind, was gone: it had become selfish and grovelling; yet, because of its very deterioration, the more dangerous. Now demagogues appeared upon the stage, . . . children of Mammon, and wiser in their generation. They understood the temper of the vulgar too well to preach to them of fine fabrics of society, the diffusion of general knowledge, and the millennium of wisdom and philosophy. Their arguments are adapted more wisely to that part of the people with whom, as they are pleased to proclaim, the physical force is lodged. The reformation for which they plead is to save money; it is a matter not of morality, not of feeling, not of honour, but of pounds, shillings, and pence; according to them the wisdom of public measures is to be estimated precisely according to the expenditure which they cause.

Government, they affirm, is a combination of the rich, formed for the purpose of raising money from the people, and dividing it among themselves and their dependents. Never before had sedition appeared in so sordid a shape. These men understand the laws too well to recommend openly the destruction of monarchy, and the abolishment of all distinctions of rank.

The third extract is taken from Robert Southey's 'On the State of the Poor', 1816.

The poor-rates have existed more than two centuries, and they incontestably prove the condition of the day-labourer to be worse at present than at any former time during that period. This, too, should be remembered, . . . that the condition of the middle ranks has been materially improved meanwhile: their comforts, their luxuries, their importance, have been augmented tenfold; their intellectual enjoyments have been enlarged and multiplied; the situation of the poor would be relatively worse, if they had only remained stationary, without receiving a proportional increase of comforts; but this has not been the case, . . . it is absolutely worse. The same quantity of labour will no longer procure the same quantity of the necessaries of life . . .

Slavery, William Wilberforce

The extract that follows is taken from William Wilberforce's *A Letter on the Abolition of the Slave Trade*, 1807.

It ought likewise to be observed, that they who thus buy their freedom, are likely, from the habits of industry which the very circumstance of their acquiring so much property implies them to have had, to have smarted less than the general mass of Slaves under the whip of the driver. And what is it that they thus purchase at so high a rate? Is it really freedom? the consideration, the security, equal rights, equal laws, and all the other blessings which the word liberty conveys to our minds? No: but degradation and insecurity; the admission into a class of beings whose inadequate protection, by the law and the public force of the community, is not in some measure compensated by the interest which their owner feels in the preservation of his property. They are still of the inferior cast, and must for ever continue of it – a set of beings, as Mr Edwards himself informs us, 'wretched in themselves and useless to the Public. These unhappy people are a burthen and a reproach to society. It very frequently happens that the lowest white person, considering himself as greatly superior to the richest and best educated free man of colour, will disdain to associate with a person of the latter description.'* 'No wonder that, as it is added, their spirits seem to sink under the consciousness of their condition.' . . .

Here again an immense field opens to our view. But I must take a most hasty survey of it; otherwise it would be no difficult task to prove, that the Slave Trade, and the system of management with which it is intimately associated, has, in various ways, tended to this unprosperous issue. The eyes of the public have been dazzled by the sight of some splendid fortunes, which, it is understood, have been rapidly acquired; while the liberal, not to say profuse, tempers and habits of the West Indian gentlemen, tempers and habits naturally generated by a system of slavery, as well as by a tropical climate, and which are powerfully promoted by the prodigious variations in the annual returns of their estates, tend to keep up the delusion.

But West Indian speculations, which have often been called a lottery, are, like the lottery, on the whole a very losing game. This will be the more readily assented to, when it is stated, that in Jamaica, by far the largest of our colonies, taking the whole island together, the planters capital, as was stated in 1789 to the Privy Council, by a Committee of the Council of the island, does not yield more than about 4 per cent; and this, it is to be observed, is not obtained by all adventurers in about an equal proportion; but as some derive great gains, others are proportionably losers. In some few of the smaller islands, the profit on the capital was stated to be somewhat, but only a little more.

The facility of purchasing labourers afforded by the Slave Trade has tempted multitudes to their ruin. Sometimes a great number of Slaves, for which no adequate preparations were made, have been put to the most unhealthy and laborious of all employments, the clearing of new land, and forming of new settlements. Accordingly, it has followed for the most part but too naturally, that the Slaves have perished, and the estate has been either thrown up, or sold for the benefit of the creditors . . .

It is not lightly that I have taken up the persuasion, which has been intimated more than once, that the determined hostility with which the abolition of the Slave Trade has been opposed by the bulk of the West Indian body, is, in a multitude of instances, the effect of party spirit rather than of rational conviction after full and fair investigation. It is in the case of the West Indian party as in that of parties in general, a few

* Edwards's *History of the West Indies*, Vol. ii, p. 20.

men of superior zeal and activity give the tone to the rest. The residents in the islands, the greater part of whom are either engaged in planting speculations, or are looking forward to such speculations, are the real instigators of the opposition. The West Indian merchants lend them their zealous and powerful aid; and the proprietors in this country head the party, partly from an implicit confidence in the judgment of others, partly from a liberal feeling, which renders them unwilling to desert the cause of their fellow planters abroad; and if they take any share at all in the contest, their rank and fortune render it natural for them to take the lead . . .

For men to emancipate themselves from this bondage, it requires not so much an uncommon degree of judgment and foresight, not even so much of impartiality and candour, as it calls for such a share of firmness and independence of mind as rarely indeed falls to the lot of men in any times, and less than almost in any other, in our own, in which fashion and party rule with such a rigorous despotism, as if it were to revenge on us our not submitting to any other yoke. Yet are there not a few West Indian Proprietors, both in and out of Parliament, who, though owners of large colonial possessions, have refused to join the West Indian body; who are exempt from West Indian prejudices, and who, to their honour, are resolved that the source from which their annual income is derived, shall not be polluted by injustice and cruelty.

Religion, John Wesley

The extracts that follow are taken from John Wesley's *Sermons on Several Occasions*, Vol. II, 1834 (eleventh edition).

Sections from: SERMON LXXXVIII

ON PATIENCE

Let patience have its perfect work, that ye may be perfect and entire, wanting nothing. – JAMES i. 4

3. But what is *patience*? We do not now speak of a heathen virtue; neither of a natural indolence; but of a gracious temper, wrought in the heart of a believer by the power of the Holy Ghost. It is a disposition to suffer whatever pleases God, in the manner, and for the time, that pleases him. We thereby hold the middle way, neither σλιγωρōντες, *despising* our sufferings, *making little* of them, passing over them lightly, as if they were owing to chance, or second causes; nor, on the other

hand, εκλυομενοι, affected too much, unnerved, dissolved, sinking under them. We may observe, the proper object of patience is suffering, either in body or mind. Patience does not imply the not *feeling* this; it is not apathy or insensibility. It is at the utmost distance from stoical stupidity! yea, at an equal distance from fretfulness or dejection. The patient believer is preserved from falling into either of these extremes, by considering who is the author of all his suffering, even God his Father: what is the *motive* of his *giving us* to suffer; not so properly his justice, as his love: and what is the *end* of it; our 'profit, that we may be partakers of his holiness.'

4. Very nearly related to patience is *meekness*; if it be not rather a species of it. For may it not be defined, patience of injuries, particularly affronts, reproach or unjust censure? This teaches not to return evil for evil, or railing for railing; but contrariwise, blessing. Our blessed Lord himself seems to place a peculiar value upon this temper. This he peculiarly calls us to learn of him, if we would find rest for our souls.

5. But what may we understand by the *work of patience*? 'Let patience have its perfect work.' It seems to mean, Let it have its full fruit or effect. And what is the fruit which the Spirit of God is accustomed to produce hereby, in the heart of a believer? One immediate fruit of patience is *peace*; a sweet tranquillity of mind, a serenity of spirit, which can never be found unless where patience reigns. And this peace often rises into joy. Even in the midst of various temptations, those that are enabled *in patience to possess their souls*, can witness, not only quietness of spirit, but triumph and exultation. This both

> 'Lays the rough paths of peevish nature even,
> And opens in each breast a little heaven.'

Sections from: SERMON XCIX

ON FAMILY RELIGION

As for me and my house, we will serve the Lord. – JOSHUA xxiv. 15

3. On the contrary, what will the consequence be, if they do not adopt this resolution? – if family religion be neglected – if care be not taken of the rising generation? Will not the present revival of religion, in a short time, die away? Will it not be, as the historian speaks of the Roman state in its infancy, *res unius ætatis*? an event that has its beginning and end within the space of one generation? Will it not be a confirmation of that melancholy remark of Luther, That 'a revival of religion never lasts

longer than one generation?' By a generation (as he explains himself) he means thirty years. But, blessed be God, this remark does not hold, with regard to the present instance; seeing this revival, from its rise in the year 1729, has already lasted above fifty years . . .

II. 'I and my house will serve the Lord,' will every real Christian say. But who are included in that expression, *My house*? This is the next point to be considered.

1. The person in your house that claims your first and nearest attention, is, undoubtedly, your wife; seeing you are to love her, even as Christ hath loved the church, when he laid down his life for it, that he might 'purify it to himself, and render it a glorious church, not having spot or wrinkle, or any such thing.' The same end is every husband to pursue, in all his intercourse with his wife; to use every possible mean, that she may be freed from every spot, and may walk unblameable in love.

2. Next to your wife, your children; immortal spirits whom God hath, for a time, entrusted to your care, that you may train them up in all holiness, and fit them for the enjoyment of God in eternity. This is a glorious and important trust; seeing one soul is of more value than all the world beside. Every child, therefore, you are to watch over with the utmost care, that when you are called to give an account of each to the Father of spirits, you may give your account with joy and not with grief.

3. Your servants, of whatever kind, you are to look upon as a kind of *secondary children*; these likewise, God has committed to your charge, as one that must give an account; for every one under your roof that has a soul to be saved, is under your care: not only indentured servants, who are legally engaged to remain with you for a term of years: not only hired servants, whether they voluntarily contract for a longer or shorter time; but also those who serve you by the week or day; for these too are, in a measure, delivered into your hands.

3. *Mansfield Park:* A Reading

Mansfield Park and Its Environs, Literal and Symbolic

After the wit and vivacity of her earlier heroines, how could Jane Austen have created Fanny Price? A Christian heroine, submissive, physically delicate and all too collusive with the privileged world of Mansfield Park, displaces the energy and vitality of Mary Crawford: so the argument about Fanny often runs. Such an argument does not do justice to the way in which Fanny changes as the novel proceeds, nor to the occasional criticisms of her which occur. More importantly, it ignores the title of the novel. Jane Austen did not call the novel *Fanny Price*; nor did she call it by any of those general qualities which suggest the main character's faults and virtues. She called it *Mansfield Park*, a proper noun which calls attention to itself, particularly when we remember how meticulously Edmund calls Fanny to account for using words 'improperly' and inexactly (p. 23), for the title refers to a property and not to a person. Whether Mansfield Park represents something above and beyond the people living in it, and who exactly is entitled to it, is one of the preoccupations of the novel. The name of the novel actually puns on the narrative and legal meaning of 'title'. So it is proper to begin with a consideration of Mansfield Park the establishment, what it means to the characters in the novel and what it means to the narrative trajectory of the novel, for the property, Mansfield Park, can mean a number of things to different characters and yet possess a quite other significance within the text as a whole. Indeed, the novel exploits the difference between individual perceptions of Mansfield Park and a significance gradually disclosed in the text.

Mansfield Park is in Northamptonshire, the country property of a baronet, Sir Thomas Bertram, and is the place where most of the action occurs. It is also a country property described at a very particular moment in time. Working on her novel in 1813, Jane Austen opens it by writing that 'About thirty years ago' Sir Thomas married his not very affluent wife, that is, in about 1783. Most of the action of the novel takes place when Fanny is eighteen. Her mother married, it seems, subsequently to Lady Bertram, and since Fanny is not the eldest child, the major part of the action seems to be set just after the turn of the century, around 1803 to 1806, probably not much later than 1806, since Fanny asks Sir Thomas a question about the slave trade after his return from Antigua and we know that the slave trade was abolished in 1807. So Jane Austen is describing a Mansfield Park which is almost contemporary with her.

There is nowhere a formal description of Mansfield Park. Its grandeur terrifies Fanny and 'The rooms were too large for her to move in with ease' (p. 14), surely a psychological account as much as a literal one. Gradually, with the meticulous subtlety and unobtrusiveness which characterizes Jane Austen's mature novels, the spaces of the house become evident, and it is in terms of the demarcations of space and spatial limits that we hear of the house and its nature. Fanny is assigned an attic as her bedroom, adjacent to the house maids and the governess, who laugh at her clothes and whose province the attics are – inferior social space.

When Edmund finds her crying on the attic stair he takes her into the park to hear her troubles and thence into the breakfast room so that she can write a letter home. It is as if he is enabling her to colonize the spaces of the house. The territory shifts to the drawing-room, the best room in the house, where, significantly, it is the Bertram girls who tell tales of Fanny's inadequate education. Her class inferiority is revealed in her naming of spaces: he calls the Isle of Wight the 'island' and mistakes Ireland for it. On her sofa, for Lady Bertram has deliberately reduced her own space to this piece of furniture, their mother hears of these inadequacies indulgently. When Sir Thomas departs to Antigua we hear that Fanny can ride in the park, though her horse is Edmund's. She is not eligible to go to dinner with the Grants but Edmund assumes that she has a 'free . . . command' (p. 24) of the park and garden. Whether this is really the case is doubtful, for we hear subsequently that she has exhausted herself cutting roses under Mrs Norris's command in the heat of the day in the rose garden – and another of the privileged spaces of a country mansion opens in the novel. When the play is being rehearsed more spaces open up and are taken over by the Bertram children – the billiard room, which is used as a theatre, and the inner sanctum of the house, Sir Thomas's private room, which is used as a dressing-room. The extent of the house unfolds as Sir Thomas's children take it over.

When Mary Crawford considers Mansfield Park she thinks of it entirely in terms of its economic and social status: 'a park, a real park five miles round, a spacious modern-built house, so well placed and well screened as to deserve to be in any collection of engravings of gentlemen's seats in the kingdom, and wanting only to be completely new furnished' (p. 41). She is trying to assess the potential worth of Thomas Bertram, the elder son, whom she determines at first to marry. However, her guesses at the secrets of wealth actually indicate a number of questions about which the text itself is very secretive. To begin with, although Mansfield Park might 'deserve' to be in a collection of engravings of country seats, significantly, it is not. This, together with the information that it is a 'modern-built' house, suggests that the Bertram wealth may be comparatively recent. We do not know whether Sir Thomas is the first baronet or what the origins of his wealth are. Quite a number of facts are 'well screened' in this novel. We know that a large part of his wealth is tied up in (presumably) sugar plantations in Antigua and that it is at risk. He has sent his sons to Eton and Oxford, as any aristocrat would, but he is embarrassed by his eldest son's debts to the extent of having to limit Edmund's living as a clergyman to Thornton Lacey. Edmund tells Mary that he has no rich uncle or relation who will leave an inheritance to him. When Henry Crawford comes upon Thornton Lacey by accident at the stage when he is beginning to fall in love with Fanny, he remarks that the house looks as if it might have been inhabited by a country family of good standing for two hundred years in such a way as to suggest that no Bertram or no branch of the family has ever lived there. Sir Thomas Bertram has influence enough to help Fanny's brother William in his naval career, but he is explicit to Fanny that Henry's uncle, the Admiral, can achieve promotion for William where his 'influence' would always be doubtful. This is one of the few pieces of information we have from his lips. Lady Bertram assumes that the family wealth is immutable and Mrs Grant surmises that Sir Thomas will find a borough for Mr Rushworth as a result of his daughter's marriage to him, but nothing is said about this by Sir Thomas himself, though we know that he has been a Member of Parliament at least since his marriage.

In fact, Sir Thomas is extremely eager for his daughter's match with Mr Rushworth to go ahead, thinking it such an advantage to himself that he does not question her too pressingly about her own desire for the match. It would bring him 'an addition of respectability and influence' (p. 168). Earlier in the novel we are told that the connection was a happy one for Sir Thomas because Mr Rushworth shared the same 'interest' (p. 35) with him, perhaps the same landed interest as opposed to commercial interests, but also perhaps the same political interests. However, he finds Mr Rushworth 'as ignorant in business as in books' (p. 167), in spite of the shared 'interest' of the alliance. The word 'business' is ambiguous, as are so many of the words with a semantic range embracing economic meanings in the novel. It is not clear, and never is, whether

45

this might relate to trade or to the administration of estates. Certainly, Sir Thomas has 'business' interests in the West Indies and his wealth is not of a kind which enables him to look lightly at Mary Crawford, with her £20,000 a year, as an advantageous match for Edmund. Many writers have assumed that Sir Thomas's wealth is hereditary wealth belonging to an ancient aristocracy, but the novel does not make it clear what his status is; it 'screens' his status and leaves it ambiguous. Those who have assumed that Sir Thomas's wealth has a massive and longstanding stability along with a similar aristocratic status have listened too hard to characters in the novel who believe this and have taken them at their word. What we do know is that Sir Thomas takes justifiable pride in his achievements, making it clear that when Fanny goes at last to dinner with the Grants, she goes as Lady Bertram's niece. He is hard-working and energetic, and sees Mansfield Park as the repository of rectitude, fairness, dignity, propriety, duty and decorum. He has a sense of responsibility as well as pride and owes a good deal to evangelical principles, which he has passed on to Edmund.

The value words propriety, duty and decorum are words which will be looked at more closely, but for the present it is worth inquiring further what else Mansfield Park 'screens' from the understanding. For Mansfield Park, modern and airy though it is, is also a place of concealment. There is an irony about the disapproval felt by Edmund and Fanny, trained in the concealments of decorum, when Mary puns in a risky way at the first dinner: 'Of *Rears*, and *Vices*, I saw enough' (p. 51). The pun is also a form of concealment, saying one thing under the guise of another and screening meaning. Edmund and Fanny do not know that Mary is speaking the bitter truth here, for she has been driven out of her home because her uncle the Admiral has brought his mistress to live in his house after his wife's death. The pun, some writers believe, refers to sodomy in the navy. Edmund and Fanny are certainly alert to a disguised indecency in the words 'Rears and Vices' even if they do not fully understand all their possible meanings. Indecency is one thing that decorum displaces and conceals, but in doing this it can keep down more than the risky joke. Twice, once at the beginning of the novel and once at the end, Jane Austen remarks on the damping down of energy which Sir Thomas imposes on his children: 'Sir Thomas did not know what was wanting, because, though a truly anxious father, he was not outwardly affectionate, and the reserve of his manner repressed all the flow of their spirits before him' (p. 18). The word 'repressed' is for us a Freudian word which Jane Austen could not have known in the twentieth-century sense, but the 'flow' of spirits is also part of a

Romantic which anticipates the language of repression, and 'flow' and vitality are being implicitly endorsed here. Concealment has its logical conclusion in the clandestine elopement of Maria and Henry and in Julia's elopement with Mr Yates. It conditions the way in which the behaviour of women is conceived and it determines attitudes to the play, the subject of which forms the second part of this essay.

The screening function of Mansfield Park keeps apparently undesirable things down or shuts them away, but it also keeps things out by a process of exclusion. It is fascinating that when Fanny drives with the party to Mr Rushworth's seat, Sotherton, she drives into an outside world scarcely known to her. She quickly passes into countryside which is beyond her knowledge a short distance from Mansfield Park, almost as if she has been imprisoned there. The outside world is excluded from Mansfield Park. It is often said that Jane Austen's fiction takes no account of the major movements of thought or politics in the early nineteenth century, and the process of exclusion going on in the novel could easily be set down to this seeming imperviousness to events beyond her '3 or 4 Families'. But in Mansfield Park the exclusions going on are drawn attention to with such systematic regularity and with so many careful hints that it is almost as if the text is drawing attention to what it conceals and putting that concealment to the test.

We have seen that the novel conceals the origins of Sir Thomas's wealth and the extent of his influence. But for Fanny's question about the slave trade (p. 165), which does not seem to have been answered, the exact nature of the situation in the West Indies is unknown. Similarly, it is by indirect narrative that the great issues at stake in the Napoleonic wars, which began in 1803, surface in the novel. William relates tales of engagements and heroism when he visits Mansfield Park just before he is promoted and causes Henry a pang of short-lived envy. It is interesting in this context that Burke linked the upheavals of the French Revolution and its consequences with the possible loss of the West Indies as a colony. It is as if the French Revolution is introduced at a double remove. But there is another way in which it is an almost constant though secreted presence in the novel, and that is through the position of servants at Mansfield Park. When Fanny visits Portsmouth, one of Mrs Price's major preoccupations is the unruliness of servants and the daily insubordination of Rebecca the maid. In a strange way Portsmouth is not the opposite of Mansfield Park here but its mirror image. Servants are a silent and inconspicuous but nevertheless ubiquitous presence at Mansfield Park, and people are just as obsessed with them. Some are named, some are unnamed, but scarcely a chapter goes by without a mention of them in one way or another. I shall return to the significance of servants at a later point. For the present it is enough to note that if servants are under surveillance at Mansfield Park, made invisible and excluded from direct intercourse except at rare moments and through report, there is an odd sense in which the inhabitants of Mansfield Park are under surveillance by servants. Fanny winces when her horsemanship is compared with that of Mary by an old attendant; Fanny and Edmund are prevented from continuing a conversation by the appearance of a servant on the stairs; Mrs Norris has constant quarrels with housekeepers and servants which are reported throughout the novel. She speaks of a poor family of insubordinate servants who are 'encroaching' (p. 119), a significant word. And it is as if the servants are constantly threatening to encroach, reclaiming the spaces they have been historically excluded from by the process of enclosure. There is no direct indication that Mansfield Park's environs have been gained through enclosure, though Henry advises Edmund to buy meadows near Thornton Lacey if he does not happen to own them. The presumption is that the rich are free to appropriate land – at least, this is Henry's presumption.

It is perhaps no accident that Mrs Norris, who is keenest on the exclusive authority of Mansfield Park, is the strongest advocate of concealment. Interestingly, she recommends a strong, green baize curtain to complete the theatricals the young people initiate: 'there is very little sense in a play without a curtain' (p. 138). This is a metaphorical as much as a literal curtain. Interestingly again, she encourages the licence of the theatricals as avidly as she advocates the curtain, and the very veiling appears to increase the indecorum (in the same way, Edmund and Fanny are made to seem more rather than less conscious of Mary's pun and its significance by their very sense of decorum). When the play is terminated Mrs Norris sneaks the curtain, on which she had saved so much money for Sir Thomas, quickly off to the White House, where it is screened from view. There is a just and beautiful comedy about this. Concealment is actually what gives Mrs Norris power in Mansfield Park, for it gives her the power of the watchful spy, a word she uses of Fanny's sister, Susan, who usurps Mrs Norris at the end of the novel. But it must be said that everyone in the novel is forced to watch, observe, speculate, by virtue of the intense privacy governing relations there, whether it is the crudity of Mrs Norris's voyeurism, the delicate fishing for information undertaken by Mary or Fanny's anguished observation of the growth of Edmund's passion for Mary. It is important that the performance of the play raises questions of observing as well as of acting.

When Fanny is in Portsmouth the very form of the novel becomes indirect and screens both Fanny and the reader from events, forcing them to strain for interpretation. The narrative turns into an epistolary form and Fanny lives from letter to letter. And in Portsmouth the nature of screening becomes almost sinister, for Fanny sees that: 'Betsey, at a small distance, was holding out something to catch her eyes, meaning to screen it . . . from Susan's . . . It was a silver knife' (p. 320). The knife has been left as an inheritance to Susan by a dead sister. Nothing is said about the potential dangers and violence of this quarrel, solved by Fanny with the somewhat injudicious purchase of a substitute knife for Betsey. But the knife in the Price family, that dispossessed and unruly element to which Fanny herself belongs, lurks undercover at Portsmouth, a potential threat to peace and order. No moral judgement is made. It is simply there, an inheritance of incipient violence.

Even Sir Thomas is forced to overlook and observe in a way which is unworthy of him when he is trying to determine how best to make Fanny marry Henry Crawford. And of all the characters he is least aware of his own tyranny. For most of the people in the novel, Mansfield Park is identified with him. The establishment is decidedly under his 'government' (p. 164) and his language is instantly interpreted as the patriarchal voice of power: '"Advise" was his word, but it was the advice of absolute power' (p. 232).

The word 'advise', concealing as it does the meaning 'command', works rather like a pun. As we have seen, there is much that is concealed about Sir Thomas; we may have to go outside the novel to glean facts about his life. We may have to surmise that his modern house is a modest version of the Palladian style with a portico and columns, that it was probably built around 1770, or bought, with West Indian money. We may have to surmise that his fortune derives from the sugar trade, that he inherited his estates in Antigua from a father who went out to exploit the invaluable sugar islands of the Caribbean, so valuable that in the eighteenth century wars were fought in the West Indies between England and France over their riches. We may have to surmise that he is a second generation planter who is no longer in quite the same position as the earlier planters, who bought huge country estates and outbid the landed aristocracy of England for seats in parliament, paying up to twice their value (there were thirty 'West Indian' members in the latter half of the eighteenth century). Northamptonshire was not a top-grade fashionable county at the end of the eighteenth century. However, though we may surmise that Sir Thomas requires considerable energy and skill to maintain his more modest but comfortable fortunes (the word 'comfortable' is another of the repeated words in the novel), we do not have to go outside the text to see that Sir Thomas is, without realizing it, a high-principled tyrant.

Sir Thomas has 'absolute power' over his daughters and his wife even if he has more limited power over his sons. Lady Bertram, perhaps, has retrieved her limited imperial domain, the sofa, by ceding her independence and rights of jurisdiction over her children. Her retreat to the sofa even suggests that the sexual activity of the marriage has been exchanged for her passive acceptance of Sir Thomas's rule and that of his delegate, Mrs Norris, and for the claim of invalid status. Certainly, Sir Thomas has power over Fanny. He has the power to bring her to Mansfield Park and to send her back to Portsmouth and keep her there. It is his power which creates the impossible contradictions of her situation: she is an exile in Mansfield Park and she is an exile in Portsmouth. Neither is properly her home, even though the absence from Mansfield Park makes her believe that that is her real home. 'But you will belong to us almost as much as ever' (p. 24), Edmund says, when Sir Thomas contemplates her removal to the house of Mrs Norris. Unknowingly he betrays the one-sidedness of Fanny's situation: she can belong to the Bertrams, but they do not belong to her.

Mary Crawford is quick to see the ambiguity of Fanny's situation, perhaps because she herself, like Fanny, is a double orphan. She has lost her mother and she has lost her second home. The difference between them is that Mary is a woman of fortune, whereas Fanny is not. Introducing again the ever-present problem of concealment and ambiguity, directly with reference to Fanny, she probes her situation with barely admissible curiosity, which embarrasses Edmund, disguising her avid interest with social wit: 'Pray, is she out, or is she not?' (p. 42). Trying to get behind the screen of Mansfield Park, Mary brings to light the concealed ambiguity of Fanny's situation and also the fact that Fanny is herself concealed, not 'out', in the Bertram household. Jane Austen anticipates the subtle indirection with which Henry James presents his characters in disclosing Mary's efforts, perhaps already unconsciously motivated by a sexual intuition of the close relationship between Edmund and Fanny, to probe Fanny's status in the Mansfield Park household.

It is because Sir Thomas has not fully thought through the implications of his power that Fanny's status is so obscure – and, indeed, obscured from view, ambiguously 'out' and 'not out'. At the beginning of the novel he tries to have it both ways: the girls will grow up together but his daughters should be aware of their status without thinking too 'lowly' of their cousin, and she in her turn should not be so aware of her different status as to be made miserable, but should nevertheless be aware of it: 'but still they cannot be equals . . . [they] will always be different' (p. 11). But how can an equal friendship subsist on a basis of inequality? Sir Thomas believes that he is displaying both 'delicacy' (another recurrent word in the novel) and social realism in creating this paradox, acknowledging the different fortunes of the girls, but the experiment is a failure: the Bertram girls are 'arrogant' and Fanny's spirits are 'depressed'. Nothing in the novel is more poignant than the description of the space at Mansfield Park which Fanny makes her own, ignored and scarcely acknowledged by other members of the household, not even granted the basic amenity of a fire – the nursery, the space which belongs to the children before they grow mature enough to take their part in the public, social world, another hidden area of the house.

This refuge falls to Fanny by default. It is a mark of Sir Thomas's recognition of her that he sees to it that she has a fire in this room despite her refusal to marry Henry and he comes nearer to making an apology to her than at any time in the novel. Cinderella at least had the ashes of a fire to brood over! Fanny's silent appropriation of this space is a standing demonstration of both the thoughtlessness and neglect with which she is treated by the Bertrams and her own vindication of her identity and worth. It is where she keeps her geraniums and books and where she comes to retreat from 'the pains of tyranny, of ridicule, and neglect' (p. 126) – strong words from a writer who is often thought of as expressing herself with the indirection and delicacy which is so valued in the Mansfield Park household. It is where Fanny constructs her world. A transparency of Tintern Abbey is enshrined between pictures of a cave in Italy and 'a moonlight lake in Cumberland' (p. 127). Fanny comes there to 'inhale a breeze of mental strength' at times of stress, particularly at the time of the play. The references to Wordsworth, whose 'Tintern Abbey' Fanny would have known if the novel's action takes place at the time I suggest, are unmistakable (the two editions of *Lyrical Ballads* were published in 1798 and 1800). The privacy of Wordsworth's moments of sublimity in solitude, moments at which the non-social consciousness asserts its energy and power and seems to be self-subsisting, is being invoked here. But it is not quite enough. Though a sketch of William's ship is pinned to the wall to assert Fanny's ties, taking the place of Wordsworth's sister, Dorothy, in the poem, 'a collection of family profiles thought unworthy of being anywhere else', profiles of the Bertram family, attest Fanny's divided loyalties and signify the power which has imprisoned her in her small domain. Perhaps the need for privacy and the pressures of power belong dialectically together, the need for privacy being predicated on property. For one would not need privacy unless there was a stressful public world to retreat from. Similarly, the power of property is asserted through exclusion. Fanny, like the servants, has to take up restricted and almost invisible space.

It is interesting that Fanny and her sister, Susan, reclaim an upper room (without a fire), away from the noise of the rest of the house, at Portsmouth. Fanny is doing there exactly what she does at Mansfield Park, retreating and reclaiming private space simultaneously. She is asserting her dispossession and coming into possession of territory at one and the same moment. In many ways she comes 'out' at Portsmouth, buying a subscription to a circulating library and even buying her own food, and this parallels her emergence at Mansfield Park, which has been celebrated by a ball. Though the novel asserts that she is not in the 'trade' (p. 220) of coming out, she comes out in a different way: she learns to resist. The private spaces of the mind and ideal consolation signified by the nursery or 'east room' at Mansfield Park cannot on their own sustain her. She is forced into the public domain by Henry's offer of marriage and there she gains the independence and confidence to resist the united Bertram older generation and Edmund himself.

Fanny's independence, however, is no equal to the power of Sir Thomas ('equal to' is another of the recurrent phrases of the novel). In spite of her new-found strength and in spite of the fragile resilience of the private world she has constructed for herself, his superior power ensures that she goes away to Portsmouth, and there the inner strength of the mind is certainly inadequate to sustain her, as the noise, neglect and privations of the household begin to wear her down. The effect of Portsmouth on her health is noticed when she returns to Mansfield Park. The banishment and the virtual imprisonment in the tiny rooms at Portsmouth, which Fanny at first mistakes for corridors, are actually no more than another version of the very real power Sir Thomas has over Fanny all the time at Mansfield Park itself. The brutality and the space of which she is deprived are simply more manifest at Portsmouth.

It is important to recognize that a violence is being done to Fanny. However disguised and however unaware Sir Thomas is of the brute strength available to the 'gentleman', Fanny is imprisoned. She is like an earlier heroine, Richardson's Clarissa, in her powerlessness and in her vulnerability to the will of the father. Clarissa is imprisoned and isolated in a more dramatic way, but Fanny is none the less as powerless. Indeed, the hidden violence is more sinister than that done to Clarissa. One of the questions preoccupying the novel is whether concealment breeds violence or whether violence breeds concealment. One of the ways in which Fanny's Portsmouth sojourn becomes possible at all is simply that the Mansfield Park family draw a veil over its damaging consequences for Fanny: 'and though Sir Thomas, had he known all, might have thought his niece in the most promising way of being starved, both mind and body, into a much juster value for Mr Crawford's good company and good fortune, he would probably have feared to push his experiment farther, lest she might die under the cure' (p. 342). These words are fiercely accurate: Fanny is being starved into submission.

If Fanny does not starve, that is because she might be said to 'live upon letters' (p. 353). The emotional nourishment of letters is a substitute, just, for physical nourishment. In one of her rare moments of detail, Jane Austen describes the fare of the Portsmouth household – greasy bread and butter melting in the sun and blue milk with flecks of fat in it (p. 363). In living upon letters, Fanny also lives upon vicarious experience, discovering what happens at Mansfield Park and London at one remove. She also lives upon letters in the sense that she lives upon other people's representations of the events which occur while she is away – Edmund's courtship, Tom's illness, the double elopement of Maria and Julia. She lives upon her own representations and memories of Mansfield Park as well, and transmits them to the eager Susan: 'Their conversations, however, were not always on subjects so high as history or morals. Others had their hour; and of lesser matters, none returned so often, or remained so long between them, as Mansfield Park, a description of the people, the manners, the amusements, the ways of Mansfield Park. Susan, who had an innate taste for the genteel and well-appointed, was eager to hear, and Fanny could not but indulge herself' (p. 346).

The delicacy of the irony here is consummate. Fanny's subservient status at Mansfield Park does not prevent her from idealizing it and regarding it with deference, even to the extent of giving Susan a snobbish interest in 'silver forks, napkins, and finger glasses' (p. 368). Despite her inferiority, she has been 'nursed up at Mansfield' (p. 342) and has internalized its protected world. Henry Crawford, whose unexpected arrival at Portsmouth induces shame for the vulgar environment there in Fanny, understands its brutality very well: 'I know Mansfield, I know its way, I know its faults towards *you*. I know the danger of your being so far forgotten, as to have your comforts give way to the imaginary convenience of any single being in the family. I am aware that you may be left here week after week, if Sir Thomas cannot settle every thing for coming himself, or sending your aunt's maid for you, without involving the slightest alteration of the arrangements which he may have laid down for the next quarter of a year' (p. 340). Fanny's capacity to live upon representation and memory, however, enables her to survive. Her sojourn at Portsmouth does not make her do what Sir Thomas intends it to – fall in love with Henry. Instead, she does what victims often do, and falls more completely in love with Mansfield Park and its inhabitants, with all those things which have been responsible for so much real anguish and pain in the past.

Fanny's idealization of Mansfield Park and what it means to her is another form of the tendency (only too human) to screen experience through selective memory, and perhaps even to create a past through memory in which experience is representation. True to her Wordsworthian affiliations, Fanny thinks deeply about memory in the presence of the uncomprehending Mary: 'If any one faculty of our nature may be called *more* wonderful than the rest, I do think it is memory. There seems something more speakingly incomprehensible in the powers, the failures, the inequalities of memory, than in any other of our intelligences. The memory is sometimes so retentive, so serviceable, so obedient – at others, so bewildered and so weak – and at others again, so tyrannic, so beyond controul! - We are to be sure a miracle every way – but our powers of recollecting and of forgetting, do seem peculiarly past finding out' (p. 174). For Fanny, Mansfield is the place 'of recollecting and of forgetting' and it is this screening process which enables her to bear to live there and certainly to bear to live away from it. Her memory is 'obedient' to its own 'tyrannic' power. It is an irony that Henry Crawford turns out to be right about Mansfield Park: Sir Thomas has Fanny brought back because his wife needs her when Tom is ill and the daughters elope. She returns at and for their convenience.

Fanny's selective memory enables her to adapt and accommodate to Mansfield Park in just the same way that plants adapt to an environment. It is interesting that Fanny meditates on memory in the Grants' shrubbery, and goes on to consider the 'amazing' fact that 'the same soil and the same sun should nurture plants differing in the first rule and law of their existence' (p. 174). Perhaps it is no accident that Fanny occupies the old nursery, like a plant. The text uses Mansfield Park to explore the great question of nurture and culture and education. How do people like Fanny survive in Mansfield Park? And in this process, what belongs to Fanny and what to Mansfield Park? The same question is asked of the Bertram sisters, who, paradoxically, do not survive it so well in spite of the fact that it is 'their' environment. The question of landscape gardening and 'improvement', as it was called, is used to explore the same question, as we have seen. The word 'improvement' appears in a number of very different contexts, as if to explore what the culture of Mansfield Park means.

If Fanny survives Mansfield Park partly by using the screen of selective memory to adapt to the demands made on her, she does so, as her name implies, at a price. An assent to the rule of Sir Thomas and Edmund has its cost even though it is to Fanny's credit that after the disaster of the Bertram girls' elopements, Mansfield Park is prepared to some extent to accommodate to her. But to the end of the novel Fanny is still pre-occupied with being of 'service' (p. 356) to the Bertram family. She comes 'out' at the end of the novel both socially and psychologically and it is one of the odd quirks of the novel that Henry, the man she resists so strongly, might have given her a freer life than the one she returns to at the end of the novel. Jane Austen remarks without irony that if Henry had had the patience to wait for her, Fanny would certainly have married him when she perceived that Edmund had married elsewhere. A teasing possibility is held out, an alternative ending in which a strong Fanny married a reformed Henry. But the accident – or is it not an accident but a failure of character? – of Maria's adultery places Fanny in the position where she can inherit some of the values to which Mansfield Park is title, and she seems to be, at last, entitled to them.

There is no doubt that Fanny internalizes the best values of Mansfield Park – probity, duty, propriety, delicacy – but there is equally no doubt that she 'improves' them in the process. She has both changed and created a tradition which she and Edmund are set to uphold as the novel terminates, a tradition of evangelical Christian integrity and ethical rec-titude. As the novel closes, and perhaps closes in, we find Susan being trained to assimilate the same duties and ethics for which Fanny was both trained and trains herself to. One feels a little wry about this process, as Fanny and Edmund eventually take over the parsonage at Mansfield Park and live within its restrictions and taboos, preparing for what will be the virtuous life of the Victorian family. Jane Austen could not have known that Fanny's children would be in their teens by the time Victoria was born (1819) but the gravity of the Mansfield Park environment does seem to be preparing for that era. The new repre-sentation of Mansfield Park values consolidated by Fanny and Edmund – stability, continuity, tranquillity and decorum – looks forward to an-other historical situation. But they are not celebrated. They provide a resolution for the relationship of Edmund and Fanny but there is more than a hint of their restricting and possibly self-congratulatory nature.

Roland Barthes (some of whose work is listed in the section on Further Reading) thought of narrative as a weave of interrelated codes or threads which change and change one another as the text is written and as the reader reads. The experiment of considering the code of Mansfield Park elicits a number of preoccupations and, above all, a number of words which have a continuing life throughout the novel. Mansfield Park brings into relation with one another the elements of property, space, money, power, servitude, repression, concealment, violence, propriety, duty, decorum and delicacy. I have mentioned the words interest, comfortable, improvement and equal, which, along with words denoting property and ethics, are recurrent in the novel. To these might be added ought, principle, credit, claim and feminine. These words interact with one another and are redefined as the text proceeds. Some of them appear in the extracts from the contemporary discourses which precede this chapter and certainly relate to them. The life of these words within the text, however, is complex, so complex that it is often hard to see, as Edmund would have wished, what their 'proper' designation is. Their signification and value shift as their context changes. This enables Jane Austen to deal with the issues they raise – power, property and propriety, femininity, education – with the utmost delicacy: it is appropriate to use her own word here. An examination of some of these words will be the subject of the third section of this chapter, when the contradictions and ambiguities of the novel can be further disclosed through them. Before this it is necessary to move away from the method of exploring the contiguous ideas and associations reached through a consideration of *Mansfield Park* and its implications and to think in a different way about the movement of the novel and its narrative shape, the syntax of its plot and the structure and form which evolve as the text proceeds. This leads to a consideration of the play at the heart of the novel, *Lovers' Vows*, and the two Shakespeare plays to which the novel alludes, *As You Like It* and *Henry VIII*.

A final comment will complete this introduction to the Mansfield Park code. More than any of her novels, this, one of the first great works of Jane Austen's maturity, looks forward with astonishing prescience to later developments in the nineteenth-century novel and in nineteenth-century culture. Like George Eliot's *Middlemarch*, it could be subtitled 'a study of provincial life'. In its study, indeed critique, of the culture of privilege it uses the rural Northampton environment of the country seat to explore how that world is constituted, what it is built on, how it maintains itself and how it ensures its continuance. It uses a few families and a neighbourhood to examine what we may call, borrowing from Fanny, the 'rule and law of their existence' (p. 174) and in doing so it goes far beyond the limits of the neighbourhood – to the West Indies, to slavery, to the Peninsular Wars. It encompasses not merely a study of *a* family but a study of *the* family and the rules and relationships which make it an entity which perpetuates itself. As Tony Tanner has remarked, the novel senses a condition of change and transition. Seeming to understand the precariousness of eighteenth-century feudal wealth built on trade and exploitation, and through that exploitation and its pattern intuiting other forms of servitude, including that of women, it explores the possibility of assimilating evangelical values into the aristocratic family and thus of making it over into high bourgeois, principled responsibility and conduct such as is exemplified in Fanny and Edmund at the end of the novel. It is part of its greatness that the text understands the strains and difficulties of this achievement and the restrictions on energy which ensue. Like the contemporary form it seems so far from resembling, the Gothic novel, *Mansfield Park* is fascinated by the nature and status of the family and the strange distortions and legalized tyranny which it imposes, particularly on women. But it also looks forward to those Victorian novels which consider consciousness in an evolutionary way and try to relate the self's history to a wider history. In a rather unexpected Darwinian moment at the end of the novel Jane Austen writes of 'the advantages of early hardship and discipline, and the consciousness of being born to struggle and endure' (p. 389). This view is associated with Sir Thomas and it has a characteristic strain of complacency about it, but nevertheless it is strongly placed at the end of the novel and suggests a social and moral interpretation of character and history.

But the novel does not foreclose on this any more than it stays with privilege: the text is less an assertion of these values than a study of the conditions in which they come into being. In this it resembles a much later novel, one which attempts to be a *summa* of the nineteenth-century family narrative, Thomas Mann's *Buddenbrooks* (1901). Mann's novel is about the degeneration of a family rather than its redefinition and continuance, but in its sweeping understanding of a family in a culture and its sharp distinction between the two generations of the family it looks back to *Mansfield Park*. The first generation of Buddenbrooks conducts commerce with a rigorous rectitude which is entirely devoid of self-consciousness or introspection into the nature of wealth and money and value. With the second generation, self-reflexive speculation as to the nature of money and value brings with it self-conscious, literal financial speculation of an order the first generation would not have tolerated. With this also follows the adoption of the *role* of the financier, the mask of conscious play-acting, as money becomes a form of representation and a risky sport. It is as if *Mansfield Park* explores the first generation and its lack of introspection through Sir Thomas, but arrests the process of sceptical role-playing in the second generation through the aborted play, attempting to divert the action of the novel into another course of social activity which avoids ludic speculation and representation, an irresponsible sport with value. The cultural and political implications are covert but immense, as Fanny and Edmund refuse to enter the new nineteenth-century world of economic speculation and exploitation and assert the pastoral care of Edmund's ministry as an alternative. The novel declares the limits of this alternative as it ends: their lives are defined by 'the view and patronage of Mansfield Park' (p. 390).

The Three Plays in *Mansfield Park*: *As You Like It, Lovers' Vows, Henry VIII*

Lovers' Vows, adapted by Mrs Inchbald from August von Kotzebue's *Das Kind der Liebe*, which was first performed in 1798, is the play which causes such a fuss in Mansfield Park. But the novel alludes to two other plays, both by Shakespeare. One is present by implication, particularly during the visit to Sotherton, and the other is read in the Mansfield Park drawing room, first by Fanny and then by Henry. *As You Like It*, convenient for its critique of the pastoral, is the first; *Henry VIII*, convenient for the strangely ambiguous use to which Jane Austen puts its politics, is the second. So the two plays flank the disruptive *Lovers' Vows* and in doing so indicate to what purpose *Lovers' Vows* is being put by the text. The Sotherton visit occupies Chapters 9 and 10, the aborted performance of *Lovers' Vows* Chapters 13 to 19, and *Henry VIII* Chapter 34. (Jane Austen perhaps knew that Mrs Inchbald took the part of Anne Bullen, who occasioned Henry VIII's divorce, in 1772.)

Sir Thomas's unexpected return in the middle of a rehearsal fills his virtually grown-up children with an alarm little short of terror. 'To the greater number it was a moment of absolute horror' (p. 147). The intensity of this horror and Edmund's intense disapproval of the projected performance has led people to wonder why the performance of the play should have seemed so scandalous to Jane Austen, when in fact they should be wondering why it should seem scandalous to Sir Thomas. The text allows that it is equally a scandal that the return of the father should provoke such terror.

Explanations for Jane Austen's seeming antipathy to play acting have been sought: the traditional suspicion of Western European thought towards drama since Plato has been invoked, and the dubious ethical

Mansfield Park: *A Reading*

compromise forced upon the individual by the adoption of roles, which leads to deceit and disguise, has been suggested as the source of the puritan dislike of acting on the part of both Sir Thomas and Jane Austen. Such exploration into the moral and aesthetic problems of drama certainly gives a context for Sir Thomas's disapproval, but more precise reasons can be found within the text. And it is important to distinguish between the disapproval of the characters and the exploration of this disapproval going on in the text. For Sir Thomas the performance of *Lovers' Vows* is to the legitimate reading of *Henry VIII* as the informal scrap dance of Chapter 12, got together in Sir Thomas's absence, is to the formal ball he organizes for Fanny (Chapter 28). The structure of the novel is formed round this repetition of unlicensed succeeded by licensed activities. In the first round of activities his offspring are acting autonomously; in the second they act with his authority only – 'But he was master at Mansfield Park' (p. 306). That the play happens without his sanction is of prime importance to him and to his children. And in practical terms his disapproval is only to be expected, and thoroughly reasonable if one remembers the results of the play: to return exhausted from an exacting trip to another continent and to find parts of your house virtually wrecked by total strangers at your own expense is an experience even the most indulgent of modern parents would hardly relish. Damage to his father's property is one problem Tom is certainly aware of. However, there are other reasons for hostility to the play. The first is simply that it is a deeply scandalous play, sexually and politically, which radically challenges the ideology of Mansfield Park. Secondly, Edmund and Fanny are aware that Sir Thomas would see the play as a breach of decorum because it involves an act of public exposure. The systematic screening and concealment at work in Mansfield Park is strongly present here. It is as if the play will be a scandalous revelation of secret and hidden areas of the Bertrams which they would rather not reveal to the world. It is not the deceit and disguise of the play which worries them but its revelations. Edmund is forced to take a part in the play partly to prevent someone from the neighbourhood entering the exclusive spaces of Mansfield Park, as an act of damage limitation. But even he cannot prevent one of those excluded classes, a workman, from being brought from Northampton to paint scenery.

With a quiet virtuosity the text puts the play to a number of uses but there is nowhere any independent corroboration of the Bertrams's belief that the performance of the play is morally reprehensible in itself. It is the way in which the family exploit the play which is the problem. So too is the irresponsibility and arrogance of a group of upper-class people performing a play dealing with class and sexual issues about which they really know nothing whatever. It is difficult to think of a modern equivalent to this. While using the play to elucidate the moral judgements of Edmund and Fanny, the text also uses these judgements, and the play itself, to explore the nature of the Mansfield Park world.

The play and, indeed, all three plays have a structural and ideological function in the text and implications for gender and politics which lie outside the particular judgements of individual characters. In the first place the idea of the play actually orders the whole book. Earlier events are a rehearsal for the play. And the play, with its aborted performance one of the climaxes of the novel, is paradoxically a rehearsal for events which occur subsequently. So an unperformed play helps to determine the 'action' of the events which follow it. The determinants of action, and what produces and motivates it, can then be examined. Secondly, the necessity of a play to mediate or represent roles which are not identical with the actor's persona is brilliantly exploited as the narrative explores what representation is, from the point of view of both the actor and the auditor, the agent and the looker-on. The word 'representation' is repeatedly used during the play chapters, both in its aesthetic and in its political sense, and the double relationship and its implications involved in representation, the creators and receivers of representation, are considered as the narrative proceeds so that representation becomes a social act of supreme importance. Not only is what is represented important but how and to whom. What representation is in art and in politics is at issue.

It is the looker-on who is at the receiving end of representation – in the case of *Lovers' Vows*, Fanny – and who is granted particular attention. Since representation both screens and exposes, the looker-on is an anxious interpreter and frequently in a voyeuristic role. As the play proceeds Fanny is almost as free as the performers: she is free to be almost consumed with looking. Mrs Norris, who has an uncanny perception where Fanny is concerned, accuses her of excessive 'lookings on'; 'these are fine times for you, but you must not be always walking from one room to the other and doing the lookings on, at your ease, in this way' (p. 138). Strangely enough, exclusion has its privilege. Fanny is free to stare. The necessity or compulsion to look on is a frequent experience for Fanny; where Mary is concerned it can dominate her: 'it seemed a kind of fascination' (p. 173). The concealments of Mansfield Park breed this need to look and interpret. Almost everyone in the novel is forced at some point to look and oversee: it is part of the elaborate social strategies of Mansfield Park, but it falls to Fanny to be the passive, excluded looker-on, passive but strangely intense, at many points in the novel.

The necessity of looking or being the passive observer experienced by Fanny gives the narrative movement a peculiar character and makes Fanny share something with the silently watching servants of Mansfield Park, who look on at the scenes and dramas created by their betters both in the play and in real life. It also becomes a subtle way of ensuring that the role and nature of gender is questioned. Some writers on narrative have considered how the form and organization of narrative is gender-marked. The onward movement of the nineteenth-century novel and its frequent plotting of events in terms of achievement, ambition, the movement towards a goal and the elimination of obstacles has seemed to some (Peter Brooks is one) to indicate a masculine drive in which the 'vectors of desire' are firmly directed towards a pre-ordained object. The narrative arranged round looking, in which the excluded and often passive observer oversees a more privileged scene, could be said to belong to feminine sexuality as it attempts to make good a primal deprivation and negation. However, though the novel is indeed arranged as a series of moments or periods of overseeing and looking at scenes, as we shall see, it frequently doubles the onlookers, so that the pattern of an onlooker overseeing an onlooker overseeing a scene is established. A pattern of incomplete mastery begins to emerge. Yet interestingly, many of the onlookers in this double or triple overseeing situation are men – watching women watching men, and so on. Such a structure means that the watched object can never be wholly seized or mastered, a definitive overseeing is scarcely possible and the roles of observer and object are constantly shifting. The field of relationships is thus constantly redefined so that the desire of the gaze is never entirely feminine or entirely masculine. We cannot attribute or define feminine and masculine roles securely. This is a way of subtly shifting and experimenting with the fixity of gender through narrative structure in such as way as to question its inflexibility.

The title of the novel, which puns on possession as well as being a proper noun – *Man's field* – seems to make it quite clear that the field of relationships is dominated by men in this environment. The male characters are strong and (except perhaps for Mr Yates) unambiguously and conventionally masculine. Fanny's subservience as onlooker is firmly established for all the questioning of gender roles that goes on. And yet her overseeing does sometimes give her power. Though masculine roles are emphatically drawn, they are subject to modification at times and through the hints of the narrative structure a questioning of inexorably determined roles does take place. The use of acting and its role-playing to achieve this is very much more indirect than is the case with previous novels. At other times (in *Sense and Sensibility* and *Pride and Prejudice*) a neat move enables Jane Austen to declare the artifice involved in gender definition. Her soldiers, the very people who should seem to conform to stereotypes, are weak and effeminate creatures. Interestingly, Mary Wollstonecraft, politically at the opposite pole from Jane Austen, had argued that just as a standing army becomes effeminate, so idle women take on the effeminacy of a standing army, an argument which is a strategy for confusing and conflating the strict distinctions of gender. In this novel, however, the erosion of gender distinction is only hinted at through the narrative form and its drama of looking. William, the sailor, is an orthodoxly masculine figure engaging in military action, the only character in the novel not drawn into drama – for even Sir Thomas inadvertently acts, as we shall see.

As You Like It, the first 'play' of the novel, initiates the novel's investigation into drama. The Sotherton episode is a prelude, a curtain raiser, to the 'real' play, *Lovers' Vows*. There Henry and Maria pair up, and Henry instructs Maria in the arts of transgression as he persuades her to get out of the wilderness without the legitimate key to the land beyond it. Mary and Edmund begin their intimacy in earnest and Fanny and the angry Julia are left out – or left to look on and overlook the doings of the others in the irritability, heat and tension of the day. As in *As You Like It*, the escape from the bounds of the social world to the seemingly free, unlimited area of wood and forest only reproduces the problems of the social world. The self-conscious artifice and theatricality introduced into the forest of *As You Like It* – 'all the world's a Stage . . .' – its emphasis on role-playing and its arrangement as a series of scenes in which characters overlook one another, are all present in the Sotherton episode. So also is the play's playful understanding of the subjective nature of temporality.

Fanny has already experienced one painful episode in her role of looker-on: she has watched at a distance as Mary learns to ride in the park, watching Edmund instruct Mary as they are watched by two or three grooms, almost as if this is a scene in a play. The onset of sexual jealousy, which she barely understands, is displaced as she finds herself feeling sorry for the horse. At Sotherton she is the spectator at several scenes whose theatricality is overtly indicated. The jealous Julia proposes a mock wedding ceremony in the Jacobean chapel, since it is clearly in her interests to get her sister out of the way with Mr Rushworth as soon as possible so that she can have Henry to herself: 'Do look at Mr

Rushworth and Maria, standing side by side, exactly as if the ceremony were going to be performed. Have not they completely the air of it?' (p. 74). The cutting ambiguity of 'performed' is sharpened when Julia remarks that with a 'proper license' (p. 74) and with the as yet un-ordained Edmund 'in orders', they could really perform the ceremony. (The shades of Touchstone's attempt to get away with a phoney marriage to Audrey just brush Edmund here: he is never as much aware of his bad faith as one would like him to be.) Out in the wilderness Fanny is again a spectator, an involuntary voyeur, as she watches Henry indicate the 'smiling scene' (p. 83) before Maria. She watches Maria playing Phoebe to one gullible and one indifferent man and she watches Mary playing Rosalind to Edmund's Orlando. Like the Forest of Arden, the Sotherton wilderness is a physically oppressive place, as people tire easily and imagine they have been walking for longer than they actually have. Just as Rosalind resists Orlando's simplicity where time is concerned, knowing that time trots and gallops for different people in different emotional conditions, so Mary, with 'feminine lawlessness' (p. 79), computes time subjectively, insisting that they have walked a mile in a 'serpentine' way (interestingly, a sinuous curve leading the eye in an undulating line was aimed for by improving landscapers) in spite of Edmund's pedantic corrections. They stay away an hour from the re-dundant Fanny, promising to be absent a few minutes. And Fanny herself is forced to enter feminine lawlessness as she comforts the angry Mr Rushworth, who returns with the key to find Maria and Henry gone: 'and when people are waiting, they are bad judges of time, and every half minute seems like five' (p. 86). By this computation Fanny's one-hour wait extends to ten!

How is *As You Like It* being assimilated into the novel? The allusions to the play are clearly signalled but they are a possession of the text and not the characters, who are entirely unaware that they are falling into one of the classic patterns of the pastoral – the discovery of the limits of the pastoral scene and the odd artifice of its illusory simplicity. In fact, the characters in Shakespeare's play are sophisticatedly aware either that they are acting and using the adoption of roles to experiment with stereotypes and the conditions imposed by them or that the pastoral is both more and less natural, more and less artificial than they had bar-gained for, and the dichotomy between art and nature comes under investigation as an opposition. Just as most of the Mansfield Park group are impervious to the splendour of an Elizabethan mansion, so they are unaware that they are performing roles at Sotherton – the rake, the flirt, the clergyman, the subservient female. The paradox is that they are acting themselves, and except for Fanny they come away with little capacity to see the nature of their situation. Both men and women fall into stereotypes which actually prepare them for blindly adopting such roles later on inside and outside the play *Lovers' Vows*. Though metaphors of theatricality occur at points in the novel – Henry, as we have seen, directs Maria to the 'scene' before them and later Mary arranges an artful harp-playing 'scene' with herself at the centre – the characters seem not to know that they are being manipulated by stereotypes even when they believe that they themselves are manipulating them. In fact, Maria, who has obeyed conventional expectations about the role of the young woman by becoming engaged to Mr Rushworth, hints meaningly to Henry that she sees the Sotherton 'scene' as a prison. Punning on the visual, the financial and the sexual simultaneously, Henry speaks of her 'prospects' (p. 83), but Maria asserts 'I cannot get out' (p. 83), without seeing that it is perfectly possible for her to extricate herself from her formal engagement. She is posturing here, as much as Mary acts out the role of the feminine harp-player. Roles and stereotypes *are* things from which we can release ourselves.

The most important function of *As You Like It* in the text, however, is to suggest what happens when a group of outsiders enters an environment of which they know little or regard with relative contempt and establish a temporary settlement there. *As You Like It* is a kind of environmental experiment in which a group of strangers enters a new social context with no real intention of remaining there. Whether it is Duke Senior, Rosalind or Orlando, they respond to the new environment by adapting to its conditions, sometimes painfully, but they also adapt the environment itself to their purposes. Indeed, many of the characters do a violence to its culture by intervening in it, whether unknowingly, as in the case of Rosalind, or ruthlessly, as in the case of Touchstone. It is through *As You Like It* that Jane Austen raises one of the central problems of the novel, the ways in which it is possible to adapt or adapt to a new environment. The visitors to Sotherton play out Fanny's problem at Mansfield Park, but with the active power of the privileged instead of the passivity of the weak.

It is Henry, of course, and his irresponsible plans for 'improving' Sotherton with the fashionable new picturesque landscaping techniques of the time who proposes to do violence to Sotherton by adapting it. Taking on the role of the wicked-brother figure from *As You Like It*, he parallels what Jane Austen has called Mary's 'feminine lawlessness' with his own masculine lawlessness. Sir Humphrey Repton, a fashionable improver, is mentioned with approval by Mr Rushworth at the dinner party where the scheme to visit Sotherton originates (p. 48), but Henry is one of those bungling improvers of whom Repton disapproves. Some 'modern improvers have mistaken crookedness for the line of beauty, and slovenly carelessness for natural ease', he writes in his *An Enquiry into the Changes of Taste in Landscape Gardening* (1806, p. 37). Henry wants to do away with the great avenue at Sotherton, seemingly according to Repton's principles. But both he and Mr Rushworth get Repton slightly wrong. Repton speaks cautiously of the 'fashion . . . to destroy avenues' and parodies the doctrinaire thinking which Jane Austen introduces in the conversation at the dinner table, which is an almost exact replication of Repton's parody. Repton believed that the avenue represented the values of '*Order*', '*Unity*', '*Antiquity*' and '*Continuity*', but he was troubled by avenues because they destroyed all 'variety' (p. 25). Characteristically, Henry notices only the need for variety, and he is ruthless in his pursuit of it.

In fact, despite Repton's caution, and his evident moral disapproval of crookedness and carelessness, Henry would certainly have found in his work a systematic rationale for completely restructuring social space according to principles which declare an entirely new account of the ties between social relationships and wealth. Recommending the removal of all schools, almshouses, cottages and farms and farmyards from the estate (farmyards particularly bother Mary and Henry), Repton believed that the spaces of the rich should be fundamentally reorganized. All signs of labour, social inequality and dependency should be removed or 'concealed' (p. 34), just as boundaries should be disguised. Whereas wealth had previously displayed its power by ordering nature into the 'correctness' and rational 'symmetry' of art, thus openly declaring its imposition on the world, the pleasures of the new picturesque are different. The new artifices employed by wealth are in the cause of making all its acquisitions look natural. Repton lists among the pleasures of the picturesque the 'endless . . . Variety' (p. 163) of nature, the 'Novelty' of its effects in spite of the possibility that this leads to 'conceits and whims' (p. 163), the 'Contrast' it can achieve by 'sudden and unexpected change' and its effects of contrived 'Simplicity' and 'Intricacy'. He adds the quality of 'Association' (p. 164). These last three elements appeal not to public values but to a private, psychological world of subjective experience: they individualize and sentimentalize nature, in contrast to the public and rational display of earlier forms of landscape gardening. Internalized individual sensation is appealed to. Association attaches personal memory to individual objects in the landscape. Simplicity exposes single objects to the individual gaze and intricacy is that 'disposition of objects, which, by partial and uncertain concealment, excites and nourishes curiosity' (p. 163). 'Screen', of course, is a technical term of the landscape artist, and Repton approves of the screen only when it does not block the gaze, as the avenue obstructs the view, but when it entices. In Repton's aesthetic of landscape gardening we have everything that Henry stands for. The erotic appeal of concealment, which excites 'curiosity', is exactly commensurate with Henry's need for 'intricacy'. It is what drives him to experiment with the Sotherton environment and what drives him to experiment with Maria.

The new affective world of private picturesque landscape, appealing as it does to inner feelings, uses the products of wealth for private gratification. But, Repton says, it also displays private gratification to the world and takes pleasure in doing so. He adds his own entirely new category to the picturesque, 'Appropriation' (p. 165). Since this is Henry's pleasure, and since the spatial and the sexual work together in his response to Sotherton, Repton is worth quoting in full:

Display of such extent is a source of pleasure not to be disregarded; since every individual who possesses anything, whether it be mental endowments, or power, or property, obtains respect in proportion as his possessions are known . . . The pleasure of appropriation is gratified in viewing a landscape which cannot be injured by the malice or bad taste of a neighbouring intruder: thus an ugly barn, a ploughed field, or any intrusive object which disgraces the scenery of a park, looks as if it belonged to another, and therefore robs the mind of the pleasure derived from appropriation, or the unity and continuity of unmixed property (p. 166).

As usual, Jane Austen's text has a complex relation to the texts to which it alludes: just like the characters in *As You Like It*, Henry is a 'neighbouring intruder', and he vicariously appropriates Mr Rushworth's land. Maria in this case is the 'intrusive object' which 'belonged to another' and 'robs the mind of . . . pleasure'. And so he appropriates her and robs Rushworth, with her collusion. Thus Jane Austen creates her own kind of moral intricacy in order to explore and question the rights of property and sexual politics.

The link between the confected 'scene' of the picturesque and the enacted scenes of drama to which the novel moves when the group of young people decides to act *Lovers' Vows* is created by the way in which the Sotherton episode predetermines the roles they act. *Lovers' Vows* is a comedy, a comedy associated with radical ideas, and again, the participants seem unaware of the implications of the roles they act. It is interesting that when Burke tried to think of the enormity of the French

Revolution he invoked a metaphor of high tragedy, aestheticizing events in terms of tragic horror. But he also invoked a theatrical metaphor to describe the political supporters of the Revolution: they wanted, he said, 'a great change of scene', a 'stage effect', a 'spectacle' (*Reflections on the Revolution in France, Works*, Vol. V, 1826, p. 131). It is the 'spectacle' of a subversive comedy which disturbs Edmund so much, though he, like everyone else, interprets this subversion in sexual terms rather than in directly political terms. The fear of spectacle underlies his disquiet about the play, but *Lovers' Vows* is used to expose much more than the sexual irresponsibility of the players, though this is part of its function. What it does can best be seen by looking at the parts played by the Mansfield Park group, which all turn out to be inappropriate. Each character in the play actually matches another Mansfield character better than the person who plays it. And so a radical misprision of the play's politics goes on. This is a 'spectacle' indeed.

Lovers' Vows is always thought of as a lightweight and rather trivial drama. No one would make great claims for it, but it is a spirited and energetic piece. It is lively and sometimes witty. It has a very clear didactic and political purpose. Its outspokennness about social arrangements, sexual mores and the equality of women is a deliberate part of its political project. The text of *Mansfield Park* extracts untold possibilities from this counter-text. To begin with, the play speaks openly of what the novel can allude to only indirectly – illegitimacy, the sexual independence of women in marriage choice, the profligacy of the upper classes, the duties of fathers, the poor and the depredations of war. Above all, it is concerned with the question of obligation – what you can reasonably be said to owe to another human being. Through the marriage contract and its status, it questions the contractual basis of relationships.

The play begins when the ailing Agatha is turned away from the inn she has been staying in because she has no money. In a tableau of poverty in a war-torn country she begs from the poor, who are themselves too poor to help her. Luck appears in the form of a soldier, Frederick, who turns out to be her long-lost son, returning from the war to collect documentation of his birth. He is shaken to find that he is illegitimate and that Agatha was seduced by the local baron, Baron Wildenhaim, who abandoned her to her fate. Leaving her with a cottager and his wife, he sets out to find sustenance and inevitably bumps into Baron Wildenhaim, who is out shooting with the tiresome fop Count Cassel, who is courting his daughter. Frederick offers violence to the pair in his desperate need of money to buy food. But he is arrested and taken to the castle. There the Baron's daughter, Amelia, has openly proposed to the clergyman, Anhalt, her former tutor. This is the part, Act III, scene ii, which Fanny dreads to see acted by Mary and Edmund but which she is eventually forced to participate in herself when they rehearse before her. It is, of course, discovered that Frederick is the Baron's son and Amelia's brother, and that the Baron has been harbouring remorse and agony about his treatment of Agatha. Frederick insists on the reparation of marriage if he is to be acknowledged as his father's son and after further agony (this is the scene interrupted by Sir Thomas Bertram on his return when he comes upon the solitary Mr Yates raving in the billiard room, Act IV, scene ii) the Baron consents and is reunited with Agatha. Meanwhile, it is discovered that Count Cassel is a cynical parody of the Baron's young self. He has seduced a local peasant girl and reneged on his promise of marriage. This is disclosed by the comic family butler, who has a relationship of great familiarity with the Baron's family and who cannot communicate anything except in verse.

A trite enough tale, perhaps, but it has some solid content. After his early betrayals the Baron does try to be a conscientious father. In spite of Cassel's wealth, he is worried about the possibility of his daughter's marriage to a worthless man whom he dislikes. He would only wish Amelia to marry him if she is really in love with him, and he hopes she isn't.

> The whole castle smells of his perfumery . . .
> and am I, after all, to have an ape for a
> son-in-law? No, I shall not be in a hurry
> – I love my daughter too well. We must be
> better acquainted before I give her to him.
> I shall not sacrifice my Amelia to the will
> of others, as I myself was sacrificed. The
> poor girl might, in thoughtlessness, say
> yes, and afterwards be miserable (Act II, scene ii).

He presses Amelia to remember that birth and fortune must be allied with sense and virtue if happiness is to come from marriage. As the Baron speaks, his dilemma seems oddly familiar: it is actually the same dilemma as that experienced by Sir Thomas Bertram in *Mansfield Park*. The marriage of Maria and Mr Rushworth fills him with exactly the same uneasiness as a father. But Sir Thomas does not act with the same rectitude and integrity as the Baron. Anxious for the material benefits of the match in spite of his doubts, Sir Thomas does not press Maria sufficiently hard about her feelings for Mr Rushworth. He does not advocate caution and is secretly relieved when the marriage goes ahead.

The Baron need not have worried about the danger to his daughter.

Amelia is in love with Anhalt. She does not see marriage as a financial contract and makes her feelings clear to the clergyman in the scene of comic frankness which so alarms Fanny. 'The whole subject of it was love – a marriage of love was to be described by the gentleman, and very little short of a declaration of love be made by the lady' (p. 139).

Fanny's shocked euphemism actually misrepresents both the bravura comedy and the frankness of the love scene. Amelia forces Anhalt into a confession of love and even suggests that she can reverse roles and become the 'tutoress' of Anhalt in the art of love: 'None but a woman can teach the science of herself.' She is uninterested in dependent relationships and takes the lead robustly when it comes to telling the news to her father, again reversing the usual convention in which the lover requests the hand of the daughter in marriage. For she is a Rousseauesque child. She has been brought up on principles of openness and freedom which were popularly associated with Rousseau (popularly associated, for his attitude to women's education was actually very restricted, as Mary Wollstonecraft knew – this play simplifies the situation). Above all, Amelia has been taught to tell the truth about her emotions: her father 'has commanded me never to conceal or disguise the truth. I will propose it to him. The subject of the count will force me to speak plainly, and this will be the most proper time, while he can compare the merit of you both.' Again, the contrast with Sir Thomas Bertram and his children here is apparent. Where Amelia does not 'conceal or disguise the truth', Sir Thomas's children do not open the 'flow' of their spirits towards him and these are 'repressed' in his company.

The radicalism of *Lovers' Vows* may be naïve but it offers a critique of the concealments and evasions which seem to belong structurally to the life of Mansfield Park. By the method of concealment which marks the narrative as well as the form of life at Mansfield Park, the text cunningly deploys *Lovers' Vows* to make an antithetical reading of the dominant patterns of behaviour and thought which condition the Mansfield Park environment. There are other kinds of critique, or elements which become critique when associated with Mansfield Park, and at this point it is appropriate to mention Count Cassel. Just as Henry pursues the delights of 'intricacy' in the picturesque, an analogue of his sexual life, Cassel pursues the pleasures of sexual 'intrigue'. He tells Amelia (Act I, scene ii) that love exists only in barbarous countries, a sort of primitive other, and that the 'whole system has exploded in places that are civilized countries', and when she requests to know what is now substituted for love he answers 'Intrigue'. The play is at its strongest where his rationally unscrupulous account of sexual relations is concerned. Amelia learns that he has boasted of his conquests: 'Made vows of love to so many women, that, on his marriage with me, a hundred female hearts will at least be broken' (Act IV, scene ii). She turns the tables neatly on this view of 'civilized' behaviour by calling these 'barbarous deeds'. When the Baron confronts Cassel with the accusation, 'the act is so "atrocious"', Cassel breaks in, 'But nothing new'. He justifies himself by taking the terms of the play and turning them upside down. Seduction can be 'palliated' because for some people it is natural and therefore a truthful representation of their character – so he is Rousseauian freedom in another form:

> But in a gay, lively, inconsiderate, flimsy,
> frivolous coxcomb, such as myself, it is
> excusable; for me to keep my word to a
> woman would be deceit: 'tis not expected of
> me. It is my character to break oaths in
> love . . . (Act IV, scene ii).

Cassel, Henry's double, declares an explicit sexual freedom and exploitation which is only hinted at in *Mansfield Park*. It is Mary who voices the belief that her brother is 'not expected' to be other than promiscuous when she talks about his affairs with Mrs Grant.

If the play is an alternative radical reading of their lives, the characters in *Mansfield Park* read it in a different way. Its subversiveness is taken as an opportunity to subvert the constraints they experience. Hence they seize upon roles which are inappropriate to them. But this has the odd effect of exposing the manipulations and fantasies which seethe as the play proceeds. Mr Rushworth, for instance, may be the 'ape' of a son-in-law the Baron thinks Cassel would be in reality as well as in the play. But he is grotesquely miscast as the confident, experienced seducer. Maria thinks him sexually inept. It is Henry who actually matches this part to perfection. Poor Rushworth wants to be a Henry by vicariously taking on the attributes of his rival. Henry, on the other hand, never once thinks of playing himself but is ludicrously cast as the loyal soldier son (we remember his pang of envy when William describes his own war career later in the novel). Frederick's filial attachment and heroism is idealized in the play. It is hard to imagine Henry uttering such words as 'Oh! You are near to fainting. Your eyes are cast down. What's the matter? Speak, mother' (Act I, scene i) without a sense of burlesque. Henry seizes this part opportunistically in order to get as much physical contact with Maria as possible under the disguise of acting her son – it is the only part in the play which allows of direct bodily contact between

the actors. Mary, aware of Mr Rushworth's jealousy and growing suspicion, relates to Fanny that she allayed his fears by emphasizing the
'maternal' nature of the part: 'We shall have an excellent Agatha, there
is something so *maternal* in her manner, so completely *maternal* in her
voice and countenance' (p. 140). Mary obviously expects Fanny to appreci-
ate the falsity and innuendo of her remark, but she fails to realize that if
Maria really is convincingly maternal the situation looks even odder
than the romantic liaison being developed through the couples' manipulation of the parts for their own purposes. The curious prospect of
Henry seducing his own mother brings out the latent oedipal element in
his compulsive womanizing and reminds us that he actually had no
mother. He is the third orphan in the novel. True to the way in which
Jane Austen manipulates *Lovers' Vows* so that it opens up the inversions
and transgressive desire of the dream, Henry has found his mother but
lost his father in the play/dream; in life itself he has lost his mother but
has a father-figure of a kind – the Admiral. But then another inversion is
effected, for the father Frederick finds is a loving father-figure, in
comparison with Henry's real-life father-figure, who invites his mistress
into the house without compunction after his wife's death and, unlike
the Baron, has no pangs of remorse whatever. So complex is the relation
between the two texts that though *Lovers' Vows* acts as a subversive,
radical critique of the events and values of the novel, *Mansfield Park* in
its turn shows up the conventionalities of a play which deals in rather
naïve stock figures such as the repentant father.

The intertwining of the two texts is achieved with such virtuosity that
they seem to be constantly challenging and modifying one another. An
important result of this interrelationship between play and fiction is that
one begins to ask, what is the relation between role and reality? Is there a
'real' Henry? Certainly Henry changes sufficiently in the rest of the novel
to make this a vexed question. He does demonstrate some of the warmth
and integrity of Frederick when he rescues Fanny, or tries to rescue her,
at Portsmouth, just as the play Henry rescues Agatha. It is Fanny's
intransigent refusal to see him as anything but a rake which actually
confirms him in that role. And, true to this view of him, he does finally
do what he used his role in the play to achieve – he seduces Maria and
elopes with her.

Unsuitable though the role of mother seems to be for Maria, it is
interesting that by acting the mother she displaces and usurps the role of
her own mother-figure much as she disregards her own mother in the
non-play of the novel. Her single-minded pursuit of Henry in the
play/dream, her violent competition with Julia and her ruthless

elimination of her sister as rival do not seem to make her eligible to play the part of the victim which Agatha so conspicuously fills – a poor servant girl seduced by the young man of the house. Yet there is a way in which Maria is conspicuously a victim without understanding that she is. The very sentimental stereotype of the play exposes the coercions by which she is subjugated. When Sir Thomas leaves for Antigua, Jane Austen as narrator remarks, in one of the rare moments when the narrator speaks in a recognizable voice, that his daughters are rather to be pitied for their lack of regret for his absence than vilified for it. Maria is caught in conventional expectations about marriage which make her more than vulnerable to the designs of Henry. Ultimately, she does do what in the play Agatha did – she allows herself to be seduced by a persuasive young man. The unacted play seems to predetermine the material actions of the rest of the novel. Where moral responsibility lies and what the determinants of action are are things made complex by the lurking presence of the play in the novel.

Mary and Amelia seem much more closely matched at first glance. Amelia is witty, charming and independent. It would not be difficult to imagine Mary managing the indirection of Amelia's answers to her father when he tries, with equal indirection, to discover whether the Count fills her with the trembling and fear of love: 'Once at a ball he trod on my foot; and I was so afraid he should tread upon me again' (Act II, scene ii). Amelia does not allow anyone to tread on her, and neither does Mary. But there the resemblance ends. While Amelia, in her flagrant refusal to obey conventions and her outright proposal to Anhalt, with its straightforward admission of love, might seem the very type of the 'feminine lawlessness' attributed to Mary, she is actually atypical. Mary has to use the play for the purposes of surrogate frankness in order to propose to Edmund indirectly. Though the role might subversively express her 'real self', she can never admit to it. Where Amelia repudiates disguise and concealment, thus behaving quite outside the conventional expectations of decorum, these have to be Mary's strategies. She has had no father to emancipate her from patriarchal conventions, as the Baron emancipates Amelia by telling her at all times to be truthful.

The play deliberately presents an unproblematic and very simple account of free feminine sexuality entirely unconstrained by orthodoxy. Its staggeringly simple sexual politics becomes an incipient challenge to the coercions and repressions around feminine sexuality in the non-play. Amelia can actually act as she does because she is socially privileged, but the more privileged the women in *Mansfield Park*, the less free they are. It is Edmund above all who voices the coercive and conservative account of femininity in the novel; hence it is one of the extreme transgressive ironies of the play/dream that he is confronted with an absolutely antithetical and radical account of the feminine. But perhaps it is actually not the nightmare it seems to him; Amelia/Mary is the repressed other of the feminine he secretly desires and dreads. When Edmund and Fanny discuss Mary after the notorious Rears and Vices joke, Edmund uses Fanny to reflect back to him his own views of femininity. '"Well Fanny, and how do you like Miss Crawford *now*?" said Edmund the next day, after thinking some time on the subject himself' (p. 54). He invents a respect for the Admiral's wife on Mary's part to justify her indiscretion and uneasily accuses her of 'impropriety'. Where Edmund speaks of what is improper and 'indecorous', Fanny insists on seeing Mary in moral terms. She replies, and we must give her some credit for standing up to Edmund, that the Admiral's wife herself might have trained Mary a little better. This makes Edmund remember at least that 'Mrs Grant's manners are just what they ought to be' (p. 55). In answer to further strictures, he continues:

'The right of a lively mind, Fanny, seizing whatever may contribute to its own amusement or that of others; perfectly allowable, when untinctured by ill humour or roughness; and there is not a shadow of either in the countenance or manner of Miss Crawford, nothing sharp, or loud, or coarse. She is perfectly feminine, except in the instances we have been speaking of . . .'

Having formed her mind and gained her affections, he had a good chance of her [Fanny] thinking like him.

Edmund's language is one of coercive imperatives – ought, allowable. He speaks of what is 'perfectly feminine' in negatives. Women should not be ill humoured or rough, sharp, loud or coarse! The battery of qualities actually calls up the fear that women might be just this. Edmund does not express the hidden positives of these negative qualities; he rather thinks of their opposites – good humoured, gentle, sweet, quiet, refined. These are all the qualities to which Fanny has been trained, or to which she has trained herself. And it is Edmund who has been largely responsible for her training, we are explicitly told in the next paragraph: 'Having formed her mind . . .' The word 'formed' here takes on the slightly sinister sense of 'conditioned', particularly as Edmund has just been trying to get Fanny to collude with a more favourable account of Mary than she is really willing to express.

Ultimately, Mary does not conform to either of these conventional pairs of opposites. She is both better and worse than they are. And neither does Fanny conform. She also, though in a different way, is both better and worse than they are. Mary can respond to Fanny with real warmth and sincerity, and great sensitivity, when Mrs Norris hurts her to the quick by publicly reminding her of her dependency when she refuses to act in the play. She can also be superficial, cold and manipulative. Her hope that Tom might well die in his illness, thus enabling Edmund to succeed to the Mansfield Park fortune and abandon the ministry, is scarcely concealed in her letters to Fanny. Her contempt for his moral view of the elopement (did Tom's recovery affect this new honesty to Edmund?) is not concealed at the end.

Fanny is better and worse than Edmund's antitheses in a different way. She becomes strong and resilient when she refuses to marry Henry and intelligently discriminating about Mary in spite of her jealousy. She has the comfort of being right. As for the virtues of gentleness, sweetness, quietness and refinement, she might be said to possess them in negative and positive ways. Meekness and self-effacingness, these are the virtues of the weak. What the novel does, with the help of the sexual politics of *Lovers' Vows*, is to negotiate around Edmund's narrowly coercive and conservative propositions about femininity. It demonstrates, for a start, that scarcely any woman in the Mansfield Park environment is in possession of these virtues. Lady Bertram and Mrs Norris are discouraging extremes of sweetness on the one hand and sharpness on the other. And selfishness can manifest itself among any of these qualities, for Edmund's criteria are not only patronizing and limiting; they are essentially aesthetic qualities to do with decorum. They have affinities with the artful naturalness of the picturesque, and it is no accident that immediately following his conversation with Fanny, Edmund is entrapped by Mary's carefully arranged 'scene' (p. 55). She plays the harp by a window opening out on to the garden, which is the very essence of the 'intricacy' of the picturesque: 'a window, cut down to the ground, and opening on a little lawn, surrounded by shrubs in the rich foliage of summer' (p. 55).

The constraints on women are deeply probed in the novel, but it is best to consider these in conjunction with the relation of masters and servants in both the text and the play. Mr Yates, a kind of sub-Henry, was consigned to the part of Cassel during the first aborted performance of the play at the Ravenshaw residence in Cornwall. But he seizes the opportunity to play the most unsuitable part for him in the play, Baron Wildenhaim, when the play is relaunched at Mansfield Park. True, he does later elope with Julia, reflecting a part of the Baron's character, but his feebleness is in direct proportion to the strength of the father-figure.

But it is Mr Yates who inadvertently 'produces', like an accident of directing, the supreme comic moment in *Mansfield Park*. On his return

Sir Thomas strolls round his house, surprised to see candles burning in in his room and 'a general air of confusion in the furniture' (p. 152). But he is too astonished at hearing sounds from the billiard room to register this fully: 'Some one was talking there in a very loud accent – he did not know the voice – *more* than talking – almost hallooing. He stept to the door . . . and . . . found himself on the stage of a theatre, and opposed to a ranting young man, who appeared likely to knock him down backwards. At the very moment of Yates perceiving Sir Thomas, and giving perhaps the very best start he had ever given in the whole course of his rehearsals, Tom Bertram entered at the other end of the room . . .' (pp. 152–3).

So Sir Thomas becomes an actor in *Lovers' Vows*, watched by his stupefied elder son. 'His father's looks of solemnity and amazement on this his first appearance on any stage . . . was such an exhibition, such a piece of true acting . . .' (p. 153). The farcical inappropriateness of this scene, the high comedy of the situation, is the culminating indecorum of the whole *Lovers' Vows* enterprise. It emphasizes the fundamental indecorum of the entire situation. More than this, there is an irony here, for Sir Thomas meets his opposite and double, the father-figure of the play. One patriarchal figure looks at the representation of another. And just as he has been too lightly content with his daughter's engagement, he will go on to press Fanny to make a marriage she resists – the exact reverse of his counterpart's behaviour. Moreover, the point at which he intervenes in his 'play' is a highly significant moment. The Baron/Yates is raving in confusion and remorse for his past sins. He wishes to be reconciled to Frederick. Act IV, scene ii ends with these words:

'He flies from the castle – Who's there? Where are my attendants?'
[*Enter two Servants at L.*]
'Follow him . . .'

Sir Thomas Bertram, along with his son Tom (who characteristically enters in the wrong place), becomes one of the servants.

Such a reversal and usurpation of his real-life role could well be characterized in the language of Burke as a 'spectacle'. In fact, the text goes on to use such language: it is 'a ridiculous exhibition', 'theatrical nonsense' (p. 153). The high conservative figure is taking part in a radical burlesque. The text allows an ambiguous reading of this incident, however. On the one hand, it is quite clearly the culmination of the unruly and disordered behaviour which has got out of control, a rebellion of children against parents in a radical play which really disrupts the status-conscious hierarchy at Mansfield Park. It is significant that the servants as well as the children are allowed to overstep their places and to take part in the disruption of routine – the carpenter and the maids who make the curtain are given an unusual autonomy and the departing scene-painter sows disaffection in the hearts of the maids. So on one reading the play is an emblem of the vices of radical disruption, a disaffection which has to be put down by authority in the shape of Sir Thomas.

But as always with Jane Austen, things are not so simple as this. It is precisely because of his repressive regime that his children get as out of hand as they do. And it is worth thinking for a moment about those silent and almost invisible servants. It is interesting that they come to be given names during the play. Christopher Jackson, the carpenter, is given a free hand. Mrs Norris castigates Dick Jackson, the carpenter's son, for stealing wood as perks from the scenery: 'and as I hate such encroaching people, (the Jacksons are very encroaching, I have always said so, – just the sort of people to get all they can) ... I hate such greediness – so good as your Father is to the family, employing the man all the year round!' (p. 119). This statement reverses the language of enclosure, which 'encroaches' on common land, by attributing encroachment to the servants rather than to the upper classes. Coming from Mrs Norris, who betrays the hardship of the day-labourer accidentally by reminding us that Sir Thomas is unusual in employing Jackson all the year round, this is a suspect statement. Southey, in the tradition of high ethical conservatism, reminds us of the acute misery produced by enclosure in combination with the war at that time. Northamptonshire was the county the poet John Clare was to walk through a few years later to discover untold suffering. It is not surprising that servants 'encroach' in these circumstances.

You do not have to be a radical to make a radical critique. The text questions existing arrangements through its representation of the servants at Mansfield Park and through Fanny. Thus the problem of servitude and the problem of dependent women become inextricably linked. To begin with the servants, there are hints of hardship in the novel. Mrs Norris defends her regime as the previous clergyman's wife by saying that her kitchen was always full of the needy poor: 'It is unknown how much was consumed in our kitchen by odd comers and goers' (p. 26). Later she chides Fanny for laziness and tells her to get on with work from the 'poor-basket' (p. 60). To the Crawfords the lower classes are a nuisance, people in the way, as their cottages and almshouses were for Repton. So Mary tells her maid to arrange for the transport of her harp by farm cart – 'and as I cannot look out of my dressing-closet without

seeing one farm yard, nor walk in the shrubbery without passing another'
(p. 50). Mr Grant had done his best to screen these unsightly objects, but
not enough for Mary. Interestingly, the evidence of the lower classes is
not screened at Sotherton. Mrs Rushworth has learned about the history
of the house from the housekeeper, who knows more about it than she.
Almshouses and steward's houses encroach (p. 69). The screen becomes
a theatrical image as well as a landscaping image as we see the Crawfords
at work. Henry advises Edmund to move the farm at Thornton Lacey,
like a piece of scenery, and produces a classically arrogant remark to
explain how he discovered the village: 'No, I never inquire. But I *told* a
man mending a hedge that it was Thornton Lacey, and he agreed to it'
(p. 201). Besides the silent presences of Nanny, the housekeeper, the
cook, Chapman the maid, Baddley the butler and Wilcox the coachman,
we are perpetually reminded of the maids and nameless servants: 'Sir
Thomas was heard speaking to a servant in his way towards the room'
(p. 249) — perhaps the servant was in his way in Repton's sense as well. A
particularly suggestive moment occurs when William and Fanny meet
again after years of separation. The family withdraw to let them experience the meeting with 'no interruption and no witnesses, unless the
servants chiefly intent upon opening the proper doors could be called
such' (p. 194). 'Witnesses' has a strangely legal sense here. A witness
has some enfranchised status in a court of law. But here the text in-
sinuates that the servants can be regarded as having none. This is an
important moment. For to assume that Jane Austen is speaking of the
servants with the habitual disregard of the upper classes is to associate
her with Mary, who is irritated by the 'freedom' of servants in great
houses such as Sotherton: 'for in these great places, the gardeners are the
only people who can go where they like' (p. 77). The servants, Mary
implies, are the only people allowed to unlock the gates of the rich man's
estate, an insubordination and a violation of status which she rebukes.
But the text implies that the obedient servants 'opening the proper doors'
in Sir Thomas Bertram's house are witnesses and have perceptions and
feelings, whether we want them to or not.

The overdetermined presence of servants in the novel suggests a
profound unease, as does the characters' virtual obsession with their
power. It may seem strange that power should be imputed to servants in
such a hierarchical place as Mansfield Park, but if they do not have
power they do have voices at critical moments, and the lurking fear of
insubordination on the part of the characters is to some extent justified.
Maria's adultery and elopement is betrayed by a servant to whom she
had entrusted her secret. It is both poignant that the only intimacy that

Maria can find in this moment of crisis should be with a servant and disturbing that she considers a servant to be so little human and so little capable of moral judgement that she entrusts her secret thus. Perhaps this might simply be counted as another instance of the author's own habitual disregard of servants along with that of the characters in the novel. Mary in particular agrees that to entrust such a plan to a servant was supremely unwise. But if one takes this view, one has to reckon with *Lovers' Vows* again, for in that play it is the upright rhyming butler who exposes the Count and his cynical exploitation of a local girl. Both in the play and in the novel, servants are crucial witnesses.

Sir Thomas's inversion, the relegation of an aristocrat to the status of a servant, is not just a joke but an admonition. And of course he has a living admonition in his midst, Fanny. Fanny, whose status is deeply ambiguous, is called in to play Cottager's wife at the last moment, a situation the Mansfield group regards without irony. Cottager's wife, played by the governess at the Ravenshaw residence, is explicitly said to be a part without any importance at all. Cottager's wife actually saves Agatha, as Fanny might be said to save the Mansfield Park household. (William and Fanny agree, we remember, to live in a cottage when they are older.) Oddly enough, the crisis of mind which arises from the dilemma created by the part of Cottager's wife is exactly the reverse of that in the play. The rich are not in debt to her, but Fanny is reminded cruelly by Mrs Norris that she is in debt to them – 'very ungrateful indeed, considering who and what she is' (p. 123). Here, as usual, Fanny is spoken for, something which is done by everyone in the novel, including Edmund. Her voice is pre-empted. Like the servants, she has to be silent. In her anguished reverie in the east room, Fanny asks herself what she owes to the Bertrams and whether they are justified in making her play a part which she sees as a violation. She is aware of 'the claims of her cousins' and 'grew bewildered as to the amount of the debt which all these kind remembrances produced' (p. 127). What do we owe to those who have given us the means of life? The question is central to the novel, and no less important because it arises in the context of playing a part than in the case of Christopher Jackson, who is said to owe Sir Thomas his respect because he employs him all the year round. What parts can the rich make us play? And when does the imposition of that part become a violation of the identity? What, on the other hand, do we 'owe' benefactors? Only chance prevents her from acting the part when Sir Thomas returns.

Fanny is much surer of her obligations when it comes to marriage to Henry. She refuses the marriage as adamantly as Amelia in the play demands one. The meekness and silence of dependence which is partly imposed and partly learned does not accept the servitude of an unwanted marriage. Agatha returns to the conventional bonds of marriage. Fanny does not. Edmund, approving of the marriage because it will bring him nearer to Mary and because it will preserve his closeness to Fanny (another act of bad faith), finds her intransigent. This is a moment when she behaves in an 'unfeminine' way by his criteria, just as Amelia does: 'Such a forward young lady may well frighten the men,' Mary says (p. 121). At this crucial moment she abandons the metaphorical brown gown, the mob cap, wrinkles and crowsfeet of the Cottager's wife (p. 122), and the servitude which Mansfield Park imposes on her. 'How was I to have an attachment at his service, as soon as it was asked for?' (p. 292). The violence and eloquence of her refusal is remarkable and surprises Edmund. Sexual politics converges with social and radical politics with the word 'service'. 'Her feelings were all in revolt,' Jane Austen remarks (p. 293). This word echoes back to Tom's 'we want your services (p. 121) during the play episode and recalls it in other ways. In words that suggest that Fanny is so determined to resist that she has not been sufficiently adamant, we are returned to the play: 'She feared she had been . . . overacting the caution' (p. 293).

What acting and representing a part have to do with action itself, what representation is, why we act and who makes us act, why acting is a collaborative matter and what both makes and prevents this from being a radical 'spectacle', all these are at the heart of the novel. The fact of oppression both politically and sexually is explored through the play, but the novel does not stop at this. It goes on to inquire what the wider politics of acting are and what the nature of representation is both aesthetically and politically. This preoccupation leads to the third play in the novel, Shakespeare's *Henry VIII*, where the text tries to resolve some of the questions it has been asking. The problems it deals with are already raised, however, in the production of *Lovers' Vows*, and so I return to this episode for a final consideration of it.

It is clear that as soon as the play is proposed the Mansfield Park group already begins to act, with Fanny as spectator throughout, because in the effort to get the parts that they want they dissimulate and deceive. Mary angles for Amelia to Edmund's Anhalt, the luckless Julia is tossed from one part to another and Mr Rushworth is inveigled into being the Count. What is one's 'proper' part? This is the first question. There is a more serious sense in which this is asked, however, for in the effort to persuade the group not to act, Edmund actually asks Maria to act.

Maria argues that the play is fit for private 'representation', but

Edmund argues that the performance of a play will discredit the family because it will go against all decorum and damage the position they are supposed to represent in the neighbourhood. The 'trade' of acting is fit for those who have been properly trained for it and whose status has bred them for it (pp. 104–5). Maria is effectively being asked to maintain decorum by performing it. Her decorum and conduct must be the 'law' (p. 118). He suggests that she makes excuses to avoid acting. 'Say that on examining the part, you feel yourself unequal to it . . . Say this with firmness' (p. 118). But the excuses are a form of acting in themselves. So the upper classes act in their own way, as is recognized later when Fanny is described as being impervious to the 'trade' of coming out as she prepares for her first real ball.

It seems that we all act, and that acting is not simply a deception but performs a social function. Dressing up for the ball is not regarded as an offence at Mansfield Park, even when Fanny introduces a cross as part of her dress. Fanny stands up for the age of 'chivalry' (p. 176) and kings and princes, just as Burke did – though with a rather suspect naïveté which is not present in Burke's celebration of tradition. So what is wrong with the 'private' representation of the play? Perhaps it is essentially the sheer contradiction and impossibility of the private representation? The word representation is used repeatedly over the play episode and continues to be used throughout the rest of the book. Edmund recognizes that there is no such thing as a private representation, that representation is a public act and that once it is enacted those who represent an action cease to have any control over its interpretation. His constant desire for privacy and endeavours in 'restraining . . . the exhibition' (p. 129) arise from this perception. Because Anhalt is a clergyman, this is actually a reason against a real-life clergyman, himself, acting the part of one. He argues that one cannot logically represent oneself in the typical character of one's profession without making personal characteristics into general ones. There is more truth than he realizes in his description of Anhalt as a 'formal, solemn lecturer' (p. 121), characteristics to which he is only too prone as well.

It is no accident that the conversation between Mrs Grant and Mary about Sir Thomas's capacity to gain a borough for Mr Rushworth to 'represent' the county takes place at this time (p. 133). For the play makes the issue of the legitimacy of representation and its public meaning a critical matter. Is political representation, a burning issue for Jacobin and anti-Jacobin alike at this stage in England's history, something that must be restrained and limited like the aesthetic representation of the play? This would be the conservative reading of the play episode. There is ample evidence for this reading. But complex in everything, the novel does not stop with this. Edmund's intelligence recognizes the necessity of representation in his perception that a clergyman's role represents something over and above the person who takes it on. A clergyman performs a public role. He represents something.

The real question, which is entirely lost throughout the play episode, is on whose behalf and to whom does a representation take place? How does it gain an agreed status? Fanny's part here is again critical. For whether or not representation is private, it cannot succeed at all without communal consent. It is an essentially participatory project. Fanny is throughout 'a quiet auditor' (p. 115). She prompts Mr Rushworth and makes herself useful, even beginning to enjoy the rehearsals to such an extent that Mrs Norris thinks of her as a voyeur (a strange way of thinking of the audience of a play, who are necessary to its being, but Maria and Henry must have found her constant presence at the interminable rehearsals of their first passionate scene a little inhibiting). She ends by believing that she derives 'innocent enjoyment' by being 'prompter' and 'spectator' (p. 137). There are some ways in which Fanny colludes with the play as much as Edmund, but Fanny's part is also the genuine one of the audience who consents to representation: indeed, as prompter Fanny actually brings the play into being. Without her the play would be like the self-gratifying, inward-looking 'scenes' of the picturesque. Indeed, she would rather see a representation than enact one. That is behind the vehemence of her refusal to be drawn in to play a part.

Fanny, of course, is excluded and underprivileged, like the servants whose part she resists acting. But she has a functional part to play as a discriminating auditor who is fully in possession of the nature of what is being represented. As such she herself comes to represent the role of a constituency. One can see the importance of this role when she is not allowed to figure as she wishes and is drawn into the anguish and violation of misrepresentation. Edmund and Mary both unscrupulously use her as a proxy. They both want her to figure as the other in the difficult proposal scene. She is thoroughly caught in a web of substitution entirely for the purpose of serving the self-interest of Mary and Edmund. She is forced to represent gender indiscriminately: she represents Edmund playing Anhalt to Mary playing Amelia, and Mary playing Amelia to Edmund playing Anhalt. She is then used and ignored and reverts to her place as prompter, observer, 'judge and critic' (p. 141). But she is a judge without authority. She is in reality excluded from the performance. She is a mere cypher, her presence saving the couple from the accusation which is Edmund's dread – impropriety.

Lovers' Vows complicates beyond measure the question of what Tom thinks of paradoxically as 'true acting' (p. 153) when he sees his father confront Mr Yates. The exploration is not completed with the unacted play, however: the incompleteness of the play is almost an indication in itself that the question is being held over. The question of representation is raised again towards the end of the novel. Again a play brings together the issues of femininity, servitude and representation. The reading of Shakespeare's *Henry VIII* occurs after Fanny's stock has risen at Mansfield Park. Mrs Norris, ever canny about status, has accused Fanny of being like people who 'step out of their proper sphere' and step 'out of their rank' (p. 184). But Fanny's situation has changed, and with this change of status she ceases to be a watcher and people begin to watch her instead. The reversal occurs gradually after the return of Sir Thomas. At the same time the novel begins to be more play-like than ever in its narrative arrangement, controlling multiple conversations and a plurality of individual perceptions simultaneously with extraordinary virtuosity. It is as if the play form begins to encroach upon the narrative, opening out scenes and displaying a new complexity. Edmund's remark on the feasibility of 'an especial assembly for the representation of younger sons' (p. 178), with its clear reference to France, seems to assert the freedom which is to be found in the narrative structure. The free play of dramatic representation is to be found in the game of 'Speculation' which is played during William's visit. Like the presentation of a theatrical scene, conversations go on, cards are shuffled and Henry deftly speculates in the card game as he discusses the value of the Thornton Lacey property (p. 202). Fanny, still spoken for on many occasions, nevertheless has an audience. Henry watches Fanny and Sir Thomas watches him watching (p. 206). Later, as Henry becomes increasingly fond of Fanny, 'Edmund saw it all' and sees Fanny determined not to see it (p. 280). Speculation and representation are allied, but it is through the very structure of theatrical form that the critique of the game of speculation occurs.

It is as if the act of interpretation becomes an effort to represent Fanny in new terms. And yet, as the novel becomes more complex in its method, it appears to arrive at a simpler account of the question of representation. Edmund asserts unequivocally that he would never employ a curate as substitute for his duties as a clergyman. Sir Thomas follows this up with a refusal of the very notion of 'proxy': 'But a parish has wants and claims which can be known only by a clergyman constantly resident, and which no proxy can be capable of satisfying to the same extent' (p. 205). A clergyman's office cannot be delegated and represented. A clergyman is not acting a role but has to be that role. Nor can the needs of a parish community be indirectly mediated to him: 'constant attention' is required to prevent their needs and his office from becoming abstract. Sir Thomas sees these responsibilities in terms of direct and unmediated communication. It seems as if the idea of acting and the notion of delegated authority, whether on the part of the minister or his congregation, are permanently removed. In the ethics of Christian ministry (and, by extension, in politics) no proxy is required either from the governor to the governed or from the governed to the governor. Any substitution in this two-way process is regarded as damaging.

And yet Sir Thomas is perfectly ready to act on behalf of Fanny, even when he is uneasy about mediating her feelings to Henry and his to her: 'Upon my representation of what you were suffering, he immediately, and with the greatest delicacy, ceased to urge to see you for the present' (p. 265). Proxy acts seem inevitable, and, as the play-like scenes of the narrative suggest, the process of representation is integral to the act of communication – for the simple reason that it has to take place in language. Edmund recognizes this when 'The subject of reading aloud' (p. 280) arises directly out of Henry's spirited – but it must be said, skilfully improvised – reading of *Henry VIII*. He reads different parts, happily impersonating one character after another. But there is no disapproval of his performance: 'It was truly dramatic' (p. 278). True eloquence, it seems, is a necessity to all forms of communication. '"Even in my profession" – said Edmund with a smile – "how little the art of reading has been studied! how little a clear manner, and good delivery, have been attended to! I speak rather of the past, however, than the present"' (p. 280). He goes on to say that the old style of preaching is disappearing:

The subject is more justly considered. It is felt that distinctness and energy may have weight in recommending the most solid truths; and, besides, there is more general observation and taste, a more critical knowledge diffused, than formerly; in every congregation, there is a larger proportion who know a little of the matter, and who can judge and criticize.

As so often, the novel points quietly to a profound cultural change, the education of religious congregations through the diffusion of evangelical principles. At this point, however, it is not so much Edmund's optimism which is to be noticed as his evident assent to the importance of style and manner, the importance of representation, in the communication of religious doctrine and experience. And he actively invokes the importance of energetic consent and participation on the part of the congregation, perceiving them to be legitimate judges and critics. These are exactly the same words as are used to describe Fanny's part as spectator of the play, and recall the moment of agonizing confusion and distress when she is unscrupulously used as judge and critic for the love scene between Edmund and Mary. But now, shifted from the context of erotic play to religious experience, they are endowed with democratic meaning which they could not have in the context of the private and virtually illicit performance – though it is arguable that even there what saves Fanny from the dangers and confusions of representation without consent is her capacity to judge and criticize. Excluded though she is, the public aspect of performance is there even though it is being misused and abused.

So a subtle shift has been achieved in which acting and representation become necessary and permissible when an active and critical public consent is present. That Edmund does not mean the participation of an educated élite only is apparent in Henry's assertion that if he were to be a preacher – and it is typical of him that for a moment he actually believes this to be possible – he could preach only to the educated in a town church (p. 287). Edmund makes no comment. But through the medium of *Henry VIII* he does warn Henry of the dangers and difficulties of interpretation. As with *Lovers' Vows*, his caution provokes him to the most careful qualification. To 'know' and 'read' Shakespeare (and here 'read' has the force of interpretation as well as signifying delivery) is uncommon:

'No doubt, one is familiar with Shakespeare in a degree . . . from one's earliest years. His celebrated passages are quoted by every body; they are in half the books we open, and we all talk Shakespeare, use his similies, and describe with his descriptions; but this is totally distinct from giving his sense as you gave it. To know him in bits and scraps, is common enough, to know him pretty thoroughly, is, perhaps, not uncommon; but to read him well aloud, is no everyday talent' (p. 279).

Henry, of course, really knows Shakespeare only in bits and scraps, a fact he has managed to disguise. But he has been eloquent about the central importance of Shakespeare nationally and personally: 'It is a part of an Englishman's constitution' (p. 279). Here the word 'constitution' is significantly ambiguous, implying both the bodily and mental organization of the individual and the inherited traditions of government which are the law of the land. The political and the literary come together once more, as Shakespeare is seen to be part of that inherited authority of tradition which belongs to an essential Englishness. Shakespeare, in fact, comes to represent England for Henry in his romantic extravagance and desire to impress Fanny. But when we look at Shakespeare's *Henry VIII*, it is far from clear either that his 'sense' is unambiguous, as Edmund realizes (though Edmund has assumed that the difficulties of interpretation stem from the reader rather than the text), or that the play achieves an authoritative account of England and what it stands for. The play opens up a debate, or the redefinition of acting and performance is a corrective, or subtle adjustment, of an earlier view. But it is also an investigation of authority, delegation, the rights of citizens and the power, or lack of it, vested in women. Rather than being allowed to stand as a final statement resolving the questions explored in *Mansfield Park*, it becomes another form of critique.

It is interesting that just as *Lovers' Vows* is twice the victim of an aborted performance in the novel (for Mr Yates comes from an unfinished performance in Cornwall), so this late history play was in fact halted in mid-performance when a fire destroyed the Globe Theatre in 1613. A play establishing a new orthodoxy concerning the English Reformation was paradoxically inflammatory. It is as if the literal fire looks back to the incendiary nature of *Lovers' Vows*, but it is arguable that some readings of *Henry VIII* are metaphorically inflammatory as well. And at this point in the novel the readings are overtly political.

In one reading the play affirms the 'Englishman's constitution'. The Protestant Reformation, in which Henry VIII became supreme head of the Church of England, the abandonment of papal power, the declaration of enmity to France and to French culture, the establishing of the line of succession to the throne with the birth of Elizabeth, all these reassuringly consolidate a particular view of the English nation. The play traces the origins of a new settlement. Not only would Edmund and Henry have been able to see in it the beginning of a continuity to which they still belonged, a monarchy and a church which took its shape at that time, but readers of the novel could see in it a model for the new settlement which ends *Mansfield Park* itself. Fanny, like the new-born Elizabeth, succeeds to a new constitution and celebrates the beginning of a new tradition. Like Elizabeth, she actively shapes a reformed Mansfield Park which adjusts to her presence.

But the affirmations of the play also fragment into contradictory doubles and inversions of the situations and resolutions of the novel. King Henry VIII is deeply compromised and his situation bears a freakish relation to those of all three men in the novel. Edmund, in love with two women at once, Henry Crawford, dressing up as a peasant to court Maria and weirdly paralleling King Henry's shepherd's masque during which the courting of Anne Bullen takes place (Act I, scene iv), and Sir

Thomas, exercising his 'will' (a word which occurs repeatedly in the play) yet delegating his authority carelessly so that he might be said to allow a situation whereby a 'king' becomes a 'servant' (Act III, scene ii, 316): all three men are exposed by the events of Shakespeare's play. Moreover, the appeal to conscience and principle which is at the heart of *Mansfield Park* is also compromised by Henry's convenient Protestant 'conscience', which can be manipulated to persuade him that it is appropriate to divorce Katherine in favour of Anne and question the 'legitimacy' of his own daughter. *Lovers' Vows* bravely confronts the scandal of Frederick's illegitimacy but settles the issue by reabsorbing Agatha and her son into the conventional structures of class and family. *Henry VIII* makes and unmakes the legitimacy of issue according to political and sexual convenience. Social arrangements begin to look vulnerable and provisional, whatever the confidence with which the new settlement is regarded.

Shakespeare's play does attempt to suggest that changing circumstances produce a settlement in new terms and on different ground. Fanny has an uneasy sense that Henry Crawford's affection for her gives him new 'rights that demanded different treatment' (p. 271), and her own new rights at Mansfield Park enable her to be literally 'Queen' of the ball (p. 220), a symbolic displacement of Sir Thomas's daughters. King Henry adapts and accommodates to new situations, accepting Elizabeth as his heir even though she is not the promised son. He achieves a new balance of power at the end of the play: the deposition of Wolsey appears to redeem the shameful false arraignment of Buckingham. And the third trial of the play, the trial of Cranmer, establishes a new reciprocity between delegated power, which is now accountable, and the power of the King. A public contract in which a king is 'beholding' because his subjects give him 'love and service' (Act V, scene iii, 157) initiates the beginning of a new continuity. It looks as if a model has at last been found for the relationships between rulers and ruled and the problem of representation, particularly as 'the common voice' is 'verified' (Act V, scene iii, 175). Even so, the new settlement is constituted by acts of private lawlessness. Henry dissociates himself from Wolsey's secret manipulation of power, which has extended even to the 'private representation' effected by the coining of Wolsey's head on the King's currency. Yet the divorce is achieved by an unscrupulous legal quibble and the marriage to Anne Bullen takes place in secret.

The new settlement has been achieved by the imposition of arbitrary power. This is nowhere so clear as in the treatment of the principal women in the play. One, a Catholic, is exchanged for the other, a 'spleeny

Lutheran' (Act III, scene ii, 100), for ruthless reasons – Henry wants a male heir to ensure the succession. Neither has power and neither can assert her will and choice. Katherine is a Fanny who is a loser. Resisting not a marriage but a divorce, she possesses all Fanny's virtues: she is 'conformable' (Act II, scene iii, 100), meek and full of 'sweet gentleness' (135); yet she is intransigent, obstinate and stubborn in her opposition to the divorce, invoking the metaphor of servitude, just as Fanny does, and refusing to consent to the King's words, which are 'Domestics' to 'serve your will' (112). The new institutions are built on violence and divorce which are screened with ceremony. Fanny, another spleeny Lutheran, clearly longs to transfer the 'unchecked, equal fearless intercourse' (p. 195) existing between herself and William to Edmund, but it is never clear that this is achieved. The 'revolution of mind' (p. 326) – the vocabulary links emotional experience and political feeling here – which she experiences towards the end of the novel never seems quite to lead to the independence and affirmation it suggests. In gaining access to the Mansfield Park parsonage and to the gravitas of marriage with Edmund, Fanny is not quite Mary's proxy, but it is difficult not to feel that she is lucky as well as good. She succeeds to the Protestant evangelical line and once married to Edmund is in a position to perpetuate it. But she is subservient to Edmund and very much his object. She does not accede with the triumph and public recognition given to Shakespeare's Elizabeth. Her good chance, though it fills her with serene delight, is admonitory testimony to the precariousness and vulnerability of the new settlement. The situation at Mansfield Park is not simply a parallel to the freakish dream analogue of the play: the presence of Henry VIII in the text makes it clear that historically the tradition of continuity and the English Protestantism founded on the break with Rome, the tradition Edmund's ministry intends to create anew with the new 'spirit of improvement abroad' in the land (p. 280), that this founding tradition is one in which Mansfield Park actually participates. And it is a tradition formed out of violence, disruption and divorce. The question of entitlement is deeply at issue. What makes Fanny entitled to her new status – chance, Edmund's change of heart, Sir Thomas Bertram's astuteness in sustaining the fortunes of Mansfield Park – is very much an open question. Her happiness, her deserving qualities, these are not in question, but the 'constitution' of the institutions to which she belongs at the end of the novel is implicated in a dubious inheritance. Founded on slave labour, yet declaring itself for ideals of conduct based on the rebirth of Protestant feeling, Mansfield Park remains paradoxical to the last.

There is a left-over question at the end of *Mansfield Park*, and as if to reinforce it the play draws attention to another unsolved area of the novel. The play mounts a running debate on the duties of the King and his representatives. Perhaps William, serving the King in the navy and acting as his deputy in the engagements of the war, is the only character in the novel who sustains a clear (though simple) account of obligation which is roughly commensurate with the ideal of service arrived at towards the end of the play. Though as an unprivileged outsider he is deep in the intricacies of patronage, using the system as far as he can, as Fanny does. But there are those other less privileged servants in Mansfield Park as there are in the play. In the play the overtaxed weavers rebel, so that enforced 'tractable obedience' finally becomes 'slave/To each incensed will' (Act I, scene ii, 64–5). The meek Katherine pleads for them. The citizens are loyal, says a commentator, 'let 'em have their rights' (Act IV, scene i, 9). But what these rights are is never clear. In the trial of Cranmer, Gardiner and his allies are only too aware that rights are perpetually open to redefinition. Lutheran opinion breeds heresies, 'new opinions,/Divers and dangerous' must be met with repression, like unruly horses, 'till they obey their manage'; 'Commotions, uproars, with a general taint/Of the whole state' will otherwise arise (Act V, scene iii, see 16–31).

Jane Austen could not have known that Wordsworth's *The Prelude* invoked this speech in the great passage on the terrors of the French Revolution, for Wordsworth's poem was not known until 1850: 'The horse is taught his manage' and 'The tide returns again' (*The Prelude* (1805), X, 70, 73). Here Wordsworth conflates Gardiner's speech with a later comment made when the multitude break in to the palace yard in their eagerness to see the christening of Elizabeth – 'how gets the tide in?' (Act V, scene iv, 19). The youths 'that thunder at a playhouse, and fight for bitten apples' (Act V, scene iii, 65) thunder importunately at the door. An immense multitude with the irresistible power of the sea: the obedient servants opening doors at Mansfield Park are by association the crowd threatening to break down the palace doors. A reader as acute as Jane Austen could not have failed to see the analogy with the storming of the Bastille, especially as the Porter upbraids the encroaching multitude with the words, 'Do you take the court for Paris – garden?' (Act V, scene iv, 2). The context, a christening, is benign, and these are loyal multitudes. But both the play and the novel seem to understand that the tide might turn, as Wordsworth recognized. Both the play and the novel are haunted by this possibility.

Protestant individualism and Jacobin subversion – in England, ironically, it is the very tradition of Protestant freedom and scrupulousness of conscience, the tradition of *Mansfield Park* itself, which creates the possibility for radical free-thinking – come together as threats in both play and novel. The silent army of servants is the unsolved question of Jane Austen's text. Southey, another Tory commentator of the period, whose work is included among the passages presented earlier in this book, was equally aware that high conservative benevolence seemed to be failing the poor. His fear of Jacobinism is modified by an understanding of the suffering of the poor. The results of enclosure, he said, had created conditions not known in England since the dissolution of the monasteries at the time of the Reformation. Jane Austen calls up this time by including *Henry VIII* as something to be reckoned with in her own text. It may have been a text used for conservative purposes, as Wordsworth uses it, but its presence, like the first Shakespeare play, *As You Like It*, and like Mrs Inchbald's *Lovers' Vows*, challenges the fragile resolution of the end of the novel.

A Note on Some Key Words in *Mansfield Park*

It is interesting that in Edmund's sense words used 'improperly' are words used in such a way that they have an excessive emotional load or are words which are imprecise because they are ambiguous. To use words in this way is to take the law into one's own hands. Shakespeare's Wolsey acts so that 'His own opinion was his law' and his language was 'ever double/Both in his words and meaning' (Act IV, scene ii, 39–40). And yet Edmund's expression 'improperly' (p. 23) is itself a word capable of great ambiguity in *Mansfield Park*. It is part of a cluster of recurrent words – proper, improper, propriety, decorum, delicacy, duty, right – which are constantly used with a 'double' signification and certainly recur in the novel in different contexts and with different meanings. Another cluster is claim, credit, debt, owe, ought. These recurrent and related words are so much part of the fabric of the novel that their recurrence and their doubleness is scarcely noticeable. Some words stand out and strike because they are unusual. When Fanny speaks of the 'tyrannic' power of memory (p. 174) or when, after Henry has been forced upon her, we hear that 'Her feelings were all in revolt' (p. 293), the words are so startling in relation to Fanny that they call attention to themselves by their force. They cut across the vocabulary associated with her – gentle, quiet, tranquil, sweet. Fanny is generally associated with a vocabulary of passivity. She is a delicate child, and here the word denotes physical weakness, not the quality of moral sensitivity and refinement which it generally suggests in the text. She is conformable and possesses the quality of 'persuadableness' – Sir Thomas sends her to bed after the ball, intending 'to recommend her as a wife by shewing her persuadableness' (p. 232). Fanny is easily dominated, easily persuaded, or so the Mansfield group seems to believe, so that when words like 'tyrannic' and 'revolt' are attached to her the subliminal political implications which belong to the emotional sense in which they are being used insist upon being noticed. They begin to ask questions: when is it proper to be in revolt? when is it proper to be persuadable? The word persuade has both an active and a passive connotation for Jane Austen's culture which complicates these questions further. Persuasion was often used to describe attachment to religious beliefs, particularly the Methodist persuasion, implying strength of commitment and powerful attachment to principles. Mary taunts Edmund for his ethical response to Maria's elopement: 'At this rate, you will soon reform every body at Mansfield and Thornton Lacey; and when I hear of you next, it may be as a celebrated preacher in some great society of Methodists, or as a missionary into foreign parts' (p. 378). The contemptuous class implications here are intended as an insult, for Methodism was the religion of the lower classes, not the religion of the conservative upper classes to which Edmund belongs. Edmund thanks Fanny for her 'patience' (p. 379) in enduring his infatuation with Mary, another passive word, but her resistance to the Crawford ethos and to the values which would 'persuade' her to marry Henry actually comes from her own inner persuasion, her deep attachment to principles and beliefs. So the text builds up a subtle network of emotional, political and religious connections around Fanny which explore the capacity of the oppressed and powerless person to resist and protest. Inevitably they suggest wider implications.

Generally, however, the language of the text is not startling in the way that the unusual words associated with Fanny startle and surprise. But it is actually the most ordinary words which are used with ambiguity, an ambiguity so understated and self-effacing that the shifts and changes they undergo transform the text almost unawares. The clusters of words already mentioned are important here. Before suggesting how they are at work in the text it is useful to demonstrate the mobility of the vocabulary by looking at a typical example: 'improve' or 'improvement'.

The word 'improvement' first becomes noticeable in Chapter 4, at the dinner party when the subject of landscaping Sotherton emerges. Mr Rushworth introduces the topic. 'It wants improvement, Ma'am, beyond any thing. I never saw a place that wanted so much improvement in my life; and it is so forlorn that I do not know what can be done with it' (p. 46). The fashionable word is continually repeated. The inconvenient avenue is castigated. Interestingly, Repton had never recommended the wholesale demolition of ancient avenues: 'we may add the *Comfort* and *Convenience* of such an avenue to all the other considerations of its beauty' (*An Enquiry into the Changes of Taste in Landscape Gardening*, p. 25), he had written. The fashionable art of improvement seems to do away with 'comfort'. 'Comfort' and 'comfortable' are also recurrent ideas in the novel and seem to be set against improvement. 'From this day Fanny grew more comfortable' (p. 16), Jane Austen writes, after Edmund had shown his protective kindness to her. To be comfortable is not simply to experience emotional and physical ease: it is the capacity to rest secure, the capacity to respond to the comfort and reassurance offered by someone. It is closely linked to the word 'kind' in the novel, and always associated with the virtues of Mansfield Park, which does have virtues in spite of the power and arrogance of its inmates. But improvement does away with all this. Associated with landscape gardening it is a negative word, as are the technical terms of its aesthetic principles, 'screen' and 'scene'. It seems as if the novel is against change and for longstanding tradition and its security.

But the word 'improvement' has first been mentioned before Chapter 4, where it comes into such prominence. It has been associated not with change but with education. Edmund's attentions were 'of the highest importance in assisting the improvement of her mind, and extending its pleasures' (p. 20). The 'improvement in Fanny's age' and the 'improvement' endowed by her education (pp. 22, 29) are marked by Sir Thomas. As the novel goes on the word is insistently used in relation to mental and intellectual improvement. Sir Thomas notices Fanny's improvement on his return from Antigua as much as he despairs of improvement in Mr Rushworth. When Henry is courting her, Fanny has to admit that he has improved. It is only Henry who uses it in the aesthetic sense when he notices 'the wonderful improvement' in Fanny's looks (p. 191), an improvement to which Mary responds with the slighting manner which denotes jealousy.

It does seem, then, that a world without improvement is a static world. Edmund gives a momentous endorsement of this view when he speaks of the spirit of 'improvement' in a specifically religious context. When he speaks of changes in the nature of preaching he is not talking in terms simply of style but of a change in the content and matter of sermons. It is the first time he speaks of content rather than form, as we shall see. He is consenting to a process of educational and social change. He clearly associates this with the transformation of religious feeling and hints at Wesleyism. For him the impetus of change comes from religion and he limits change to the religious context. But there is also no doubt that he is thinking of a transformation which affects all classes. The spirit of improvement *is* a spiritual one, but in so far as improvement can create far-reaching educational change, it is not the wanton pursuit of the upper classes, manifesting itself in the aestheticizing of ethics and the appropriation of space.

We can turn by way of 'improvement' to the clusters of seemingly inconspicuous words with which this note begins. Proper, improper, propriety, impropriety, decorum, delicacy, duty, right; and then claim, credit, debt, owe, ought. The repetition of all these words is so prolific in so many different contexts which accomplish a subtle shift of meaning that it is impossible to provide a comprehensive study of them. But inconspicuous as they are, they are the dominant words of the text. Each cluster is connected with the other and it is actually artificial to separate them, though it is necessary to do so for the purpose of convenience. The first thing to notice about the initial cluster is that they are abstractions. They indicate a form of conduct or behaviour without necessarily declaring its content. In a society other than Mansfield Park, propriety and decorum might well be constituted by quite other customs than those current there. Indeed, they are founded on custom and the assumption that we know what manners and conduct are by social agreement. Thus, although they are ethical abstractions, the words declare simply that they are ethical rather than indicating of what the ethical consists. Indeed, when looked at more closely, words such as propriety, decorum and delicacy are as much aesthetic words as ethical ideas. They all suggest fitness and suitably ordered relationships and are often used in dictionaries to gloss one another. We can have disagreements over the aesthetic and that is why these words are often at issue in Mansfield Park. Thus the aesthetic pulls away from the moral. It is interesting that Dr Johnson's *Dictionary*, the most influential dictionary Jane Austen would have known, glosses *Decorum* as 'Decency; behaviour contrary to licentiousness, contrary to levity; seemliness.' *Decorous* is 'becoming; proper, befitting; seemly.' *Delicacy* has eleven meanings, among which are 'Anything mighty pleasing to the senses (3); feminine beauty (4); politeness of manners; contrary to grossness (7); tenderness (9); weakness (10).' Both delicacy and decorum can be the result of education and conditioning rather than having ethical content. They can confuse rather than clarify the notion of duties and rights and provide no basis for deciding about them. They can disguise real social situations.

The next group of words – claim, credit, debt, owe, ought – suggests the moral and ethical rather than the aesthetic, but they also are complicated. For they have economic, financial and legal implications which can cut right across their moral signification. A claim calls upon a public situation and is granted a legal status as much as a moral one. Credit is something you possess or lay claim to by virtue of public recognition of your trustworthiness. But it is a .curiously unstable virtue. It depends ultimately on people's confidence, on their belief in your capacity to pay later for the trust invested in you. And your capacity to pay is an invisible entity. A debt is likewise an invisible entity whether it is a moral or a financial debt. It is obligation built up over time. In the case of a moral debt the invisible obligation cannot be specific or accounted, whereas a financial debt is a specifically agreed amount. You can 'owe' morally and financially, but this does not always clarify what you 'ought' to do. Jane Austen's text exploits the ambiguities inherent in these double financial and moral words with as much virtuosity as it exploits both the ludic and ethical implications of the first cluster of aesthetic and moral ambiguities. The word which brings these two groups of qualities together is 'property', significantly embodied in the title of *Mansfield Park*, as we have seen. For property can be a concrete and material thing, something you own, tied up with finance, entitlement, capable of being bought and sold. But a property can also be an intangible attribute, a quality of something. Property and propriety are allied and come from the same roots. The idea of fitness, rightness and correctness in propriety comes from the sense that correctness is what intrinsically and absolutely belongs exclusively to a particular form of behaviour. Both have to do with ownership.

It is not possible to look at all of these words, but there are occasions in the novel when they are used to open up the problem of what rights and duties are. All the clusters of words I have mentioned circulate in the *Lovers' Vows* episode. As Tom asserts that the play will mean no damage to his father's property, the carpenter comes in to damage it by making properties. And parts are 'appropriated' (p. 103) or people believe that parts are the property of others, as Amelia is assumed to be the property of Mary. Worse, the idea of property spreads to relationships. Julia, whose 'property' (p. 38) Henry Crawford was once assumed to be, is involved in a bitter and jealous feud with Maria. While their 'interests' were the same, the narrator comments (p. 134), the sisters could be friends, but in the dispute over who should act with Henry they fall out. 'Interests' here has a sinister economic overtone, suggesting as it does a financial complicity which dissolves as soon as their parts in the ownership of Henry conflict. Edmund is caught between his theatrical and his real part and the conflicting 'claims' of Mary's sexuality and his own conduct (p. 135). The 'liberties' of the theatricals dissolve the certainties of moral definition, so that Edmund feels he is 'right' (p. 132) to take the part of Anhalt.

Edmund sees the invitation to the luckless Charles Maddox as the end of 'privacy and propriety' (p. 128) and is determined to keep him out (though he does actually get in later at the ball). For all his moral elevation, Edmund's language does not ring true. As Maria realizes, he is just as concerned with the family's 'discredit', as Mrs Norris calls it, (p. 118) in the neighbourhood and the intrusion of others into the privileged world of Mansfield Park as he is with ethics. The language of persuasion with which he confronts Maria shows this. He asks for 'delicacy' and 'decorum', aestheticized words which both have their root in the idea of sensuous beauty and its appreciation (p. 118). It is no real wonder that she is not convinced, for he concentrates on the outward form of conduct and not its content. Nor is it surprising that Maria accuses him of being 'nice' (p. 118), another word with its roots in sensation. 'Do not act any thing improper, my dear,' Lady Bertram calls out from the sofa, vaguely aware of the dispute (p. 118). There is an irony in this, for Edmund is using words improperly, and asking Maria to act the improper by suggesting that she 'acts' delicacy and decorum rather than manifesting their moral content.

But again ironically, since she has refused to participate in the theatricals, it is Fanny who is thrown into most moral confusion by language and its doubleness at the time of the play. As she looks round the east room she sees the tangible evidence of what she owes to the Bertram family in the shape of gifts and trinkets (though with warning significance the text reminds us that the netting-boxes she sees around her are presented 'principally by Tom' (p. 127), the Bertram male least interested in Fanny) and contemplates the 'claims' of her cousins and the 'debt' she owes them. Though it is nowhere suggested that Fanny should act, this is a subtle moment where real moral ambiguity arises. Fanny does owe something to the Bertrams, her education at the very least. It is necessarily a one-sided relationship. The material and the moral are intertwined. It is another problem never fully solved in the text. It contains itself by exploring what she does not owe the Bertrams. Duty is a difficult and exacting concept, and it is by no means clear what it is.

There is, however, one word in the text which only once becomes contaminated with the idea of finance: principle. This word is always associated with Fanny. Despite the fact that it is as empty of content as the other abstractions circulating in the novel, it is reserved for the integrity of moral judgements. Henry uses words such as decorum and delicacy of Fanny when he is in love with her because, says Jane Austen, he could not name her qualities by any other words. On her part she sees that he has 'no principle to supply as a duty' (p. 271). It may be just as hard to determine what principles are as it is to determine what decorum is, but we can see how they can 'supply' or fill the concept of duty by seeing what they are not. A few lines later Sir Thomas resigns himself to waiting for Fanny to come round. He rests his trust in Henry's continued affection: 'and when seeing such confidence of success in the principal, Sir Thomas was soon able to depend on it himself' (pp. 271–2). The 'principal' is both Henry and money invested to gain interest. Its punning affinity to 'principle' suggests that improper doubleness about language which is so worrying to the text. But it achieves a clarification through punning as well. Financial investment and moral feeling are not the same thing, even when we might be said to 'invest' both in our lives. Henry's sexual confidence somehow gives him a kind of financial credit with Sir Thomas, which is both metaphorical and literal, for he is hoping to see Fanny married to a rich man. But his confidence is misplaced because it is not principled confidence. Sir Thomas is indulging in the game of 'Speculation' so beloved by the Crawfords. It is a game they all lose.

'Conservative' Jane Austen?—Some Views

The following note on critical views of Jane Austen is not intended to survey her reputation exhaustively. That has been very effectively done recently by B. C. Southam in his Critical Heritage volumes (see the section on Further Reading). This last section of my study is intended to ask some questions about the ways in which Jane Austen has been discussed and to strike a cautionary note. First of all, why has her work so long been regarded as that of an essentially conservative writer? Why has this been assumed and celebrated, with some significant exceptions, right up to the 1970s? Why, subsequently, has this view been modified?

The most famous discussion of Jane Austen as a writer working within narrow social limits and expectations is undoubtedly that of Charlotte Brontë. In 1848 she wrote to G. H. Lewes in the following terms:

An accurate daguerrotyped portrait of a commonplace face; a carefully fenced, highly cultivated garden, with neat borders and delicate flowers; but no glance of a bright vivid physiognomy, no open country, no fresh air; no blue hill, no bonny beck. I should hardly like to live with her ladies and gentlemen, in their elegant but confined houses.

Charlotte Brontë was writing of *Pride and Prejudice*, but her strictures are possibly more relevant to a reading of *Mansfield Park* if one works within the terms she uses. She was thinking, of course, of the lack of intensity and passion in Jane Austen's work as well as its restricted social field, but her description implies conservatism in both the general and political senses of the word. Many nineteenth-century readers agreed with her. Either, like Carlyle, they thought of her work as mere 'dish-washings' (a remark of 1850 quoted by Francis Espinasse in his *Literary Recollections*, 1893) and described it in terms of 'dull stories without incidents, full of level conversation, and concerned with characters of middle life' (article in *Christian Remembrancer*, 1853), or they celebrated what they saw as a meticulously realist painting of the society of English country gentlemen 'as it was, in all its features' (Goldwin Smith in *The Nation*, 1870) and delighted in the fidelity of her art to known social experience.

Those who considered Jane Austen more daring and inventive than these descriptions suggest made an interesting move. They compared her with Shakespeare, implying a range, depth and insight far beyond that of most poets as well as of most novelists. Tennyson, rather unexpectedly, was one such critic, and is said to have rushed to the spot in Lyme Regis where one of the characters in *Persuasion*, Louisa, fell down some steps. But the sense of a novelist writing of and from within a closed society continued well into the twentieth century. Her recognition of the limits and realities of social life, it was assumed, gave her a supreme moral insight into the nature of permanent human problems in society and provided a basis for judgement and ethical discrimination which transcended her particular historical situation. Lord David Cecil represents this view most typically in the twentieth century: 'her graceful unpretentious philosophy, founded as it is on an unwavering recognition of fact, directed by an unerring perception of moral quality, is as impressive as those of the most majestic novelists,' he wrote in his Leslie Stephen Lecture on Jane Austen in 1935. He said that he would go to Jane Austen for moral advice and would be very perturbed if she were to disagree with him. Cecil belongs to the cult of Jane Austen (often nicknamed 'Janeites'), people who read Jane Austen as if every detail of her novels belongs not to the world of fiction but to their experience, people who believe that because they are at home in her world, she would be at home in theirs.

One can begin to see the basis of the conservative reading of Jane Austen. It is a moral reading and a class-based reading which are intertwined. Those, like Charlotte Brontë, who disliked her work linked the restricted social world of the novels to emotional and moral narrowness. Those who responded positively to her work assumed that the restricted class base of the novels was so natural to Jane Austen and so completely assimilated that it was virtually naturalized and provided a basis of stability and security from which the most scrupulous observation and moral judgement could operate. Since she herself appeared to ignore the major historical and political movements of her time (though I hope I have managed to dispel that impression by now), we ourselves could be justified in ignoring them too and lift Jane Austen's work out of history into the realm of moral universals.

An alternative form of the same strategy is to praise, as Virginia Woolf did, 'her greatness as an artist'. Writing in *The Times Literary Supplement* in 1913 she described the 'conservative spirit' of Jane Austen in terms of the finesse and subtlety of aesthetic form: 'More than any other novelist she fills every inch of her canvas with observation, fashions every sentence into meaning, stuffs up every chink and cranny of the fabric until each novel is a little living world, from which you cannot break off a scene or even a sentence without bleeding some of its life.' Here it is the organic unity and completeness of Jane Austen's world which is being praised as much as its ethical sensitivity. Virginia Woolf's criteria of wholeness and intricacy later led her to compare Jane Austen's art with that of Henry James and Proust (*Athenaeum*, 15 December 1923). James had earlier praised Jane Austen in the same terms, arguing that even the 'dropped stitches' of her imagination produced 'little glimpses of steady vision, little master-strokes of imagination' (an essay of 1905, reprinted in *The House of Fiction*). The academic descendant of these views is the classic study by Mary Lascelles, *Jane Austen and Her Art* (1939). In this kind of study there is a move towards formalism rather than morality, but the effect can often be the same: in both approaches the history and politics crossed by the novels (and crossing them) begins to disappear.

One exceptional nineteenth-century critic, Richard Simpson, writing in *The North British Review* (1870), speaks in terms very different from those of his nineteenth-century contemporaries, and, it must be said, in terms often very different from twentieth-century writers. This is a particularly notable achievement when one remembers that the influential *Memoir* of Jane Austen published in 1870 by her nephew, J. E. Austen-Leigh, which presented a sentimental and conventional picture of Jane Austen, was the occasion of his review. Simpson writes of Jane Austen's intelligence, her irony, her 'critical spirit . . . at the foundation of her artistic faculty'. He represents a minority tradition which surfaces again in the work of Reginald Farrer, who asked for an 'objective' reading of the novels ('Jane Austen', *Quarterly Review*, July 1917), in D. W. Harding's 'Regulated Hatred' (*Scrutiny*, 1940) and in W. H. Auden's poem 'Letter to Lord Byron' in *Letters from Iceland* (1937), which describes Jane Austen's revelation of 'The economic basis of society' so 'frankly and with such sobriety'.

If we are not to assume eclectically that these are all different 'approaches', all equally valid and each representing the different ideological positions of different readers, it is necessary to inquire a little further into these differing readings. It is interesting to note that the harsher, satirical Jane Austen emerges in criticism at times of national stress, war or danger. Simpson was writing in a decade which saw renewed conflict in Europe and further demands for political reform at home. Farrer was writing during the First World War, Harding in the Second and Auden just before. This may be to displace critical relativism from writers to a moment in history, but it does suggest that moments of cultural stress or lack of cohesion open up the conservative readings of Jane Austen to inspection and disclose elements in the texts which have been ignored or have remained unnoticed. Perhaps one could say that they hardly existed until they were named. The radical readings certainly draw attention to the fact that every reading of a text is a construction. But even if we see that readings are called out by particular historical moments and particular positions, it is not necessary to return to the eclectic position that anything is valid, anything goes.

To begin with, if a text discloses a reading different from a conventional one, that may be because there are areas of unease, unsolved problems and contradictions working in the writing which enable quite contradictory readings to occur. Most readings tidy up and foreclose on uncertainties. The more insistent the closure, the less convincing the reading. Both conservative and radical readings can do this. On the other hand, it is another kind of closure simply to say that a text is fundamentally contradictory and leave it at that, another form of mastery. There is no right reading, but what one can do is to try and determine where the unsolved elements of the text occur, what is left in play, where they are derived from and how they are configured in the text. For instance, if one is aware of the religious and radical discourses simultaneously debating the nature of qualities such as patience, delicacy and gentleness in the decades preceding the writing of *Mansfield Park*, it should be possible to see not only that there is considerable conflict about these in the novel but that they are also being subjected to a subtle critique which also has its uncertainties. This is evident from a reading of the text alone; to go outside it helps to clarify the problems further. The same is true of the degree of play and unease round the idea of representation and the idea of service. It is arguable that such a cluster of anxieties are, as it were, Tory anxieties. One could certainly point outside the novel to statements by Jane Austen about these issues which are pretty uncompromising. But it is, as I have already said, possible to make a radical critique without being a radical, and if it is preferable to see this as a conservative critique, then the limits and anxieties of that confrontation are just as important as any other. What we find ourselves doing is attending to the network of connections within the text and to its language and to the relations of that with the languages of other texts. We find ourselves asking questions rather than providing answers. My own reading of the novel convinces me that areas of the text are confused – one would point to the worries around *Henry VIII* – just as other areas of it are deeply subversive – and here one would point to the sexual politics of the novel. Another area of uncertainty is around the ultimate elimination of the Crawfords. There will always be contested areas in complex texts and that is why readings will always be contested. By clarifying the way in which problems are configured and exposed, however, one provides grounds for rational debate. Such debate cannot take place if we assume that any position is valid or that changing critical views are simply the result of changing critical fashion. One will be much more sharply aware of the ideological reading, just as one will be more sharply aware of the ideology of the text and its problems, if one explores the unease at work in a piece of writing.

Readings of *Mansfield Park* in the twentieth century have tended to try and decide what the novel is about in order to erase the critic's puzzlement and the uncertainty which arises from the difficult gravitas of the text. Lionel Trilling's classic essay on *Mansfield Park* is troubled on many points: he is worried about the passivity and delicacy of Fanny; he is worried about the scandal of the play and the almost Victorian prudery which its presentation evokes; he is worried about the sobriety of the ending and the rather gloomy rectitude which dismisses the energy of the Crawfords. This essay, reprinted in *The Opposing Self* (1955), tends to close off areas of conflict by assuming that the text unequivocally opts for particular conclusions rather than exploring a set of problems. Thus uneasiness is located not in the novel but in the mind of the critic, who is worried by what he interprets as Jane Austen's closed solutions. Trilling believes that the reassertion of the values of stability and Christian integrity embodied in the marriage of Edmund and Fanny leads to a deliberate acceptance of a world in which the play of energy and vitality is repressed in favour of the ethical life of sacrifice and passivity. The disapproval of the play is a part of that cutting-off of energy. He explains the resistance to acting as a resistance to the deceit of representation deeply felt in European culture, particularly where there was, as in *Mansfield Park*, a strong ethical code. The ending chooses low-pulsed rectitude as against the thrusting Crawford vitalities. It is clear that he is trying to empathize with a value system which deeply perturbs him. Where he can, he retrieves from the novel a liberal Jane Austen oddly like himself.

Other criticisms of *Mansfield Park* have not attempted the imaginative effort of getting inside what they interpret as its values and ideology but have simply assumed that its values are narrow and antipathetic. Farrer attacked the hypocrisy of the ending, which celebrated the marriage of a prig and a passive girl materially rewarded for being morally right: the novel 'is vitiated throughout by a radical dishonesty'. Kingsley Amis mounted a full-scale attack on *Mansfield Park* in an aggressive essay written in 1957, 'What Became of Jane Austen?'. Like Farrer, who described Fanny as 'the female prig-pharisee', Amis attacks Fanny for lacking 'self-knowledge, generosity and humility'. Edmund's 'notions and feelings are vitiated by a narrow and unreflecting pomposity, Fanny's are made odious by a self-regard utterly unredeemed by any humour'.

But Trilling's act of empathy and Amis's aggression both assume that the novel closes on fixed positions. Neither assume internal inquiry, critique, openness, unease or anxiety. Neither assume a text in dialogue with itself. Both concentrate overwhelmingly on the actions of characters as indicators of the ideological position of the author, in spite of the sophistication with which they discuss the text.

My own belief is that a radical reading of *Mansfield Park*, that most serious and troubled of Jane Austen's works, is possible when one stops reading decisions of character as decisions of the author and sees the text as an exploration of the constitution of a great middle-class family, its repressions, tyrannies, tragedies and compromises – perhaps the marriage of Edmund and Fanny is the greatest compromise. Recently, the work of novelists writing in the same period as Jane Austen has been reprinted. Often they deal with the same themes (Susan Ferrier's *Marriage*, for instance) and yet these energetic and intelligent novelists (Maria Edgeworth, Charlotte Lennox, Mary Brunton, for instance) go nothing like so far in critical analysis as Jane Austen. This is one indication of her capacity for critique.

The reading of Jane Austen which challenges the conservative view has emerged concurrently with accounts of the text and the act of reading which explore the possibility of seeing the text in terms of critique. In very different ways Marxism and deconstruction enable this kind of reading. That is why it might be more useful for the new reader of Jane Austen to look at Barthes's *S/Z* (1974) or Bakhtin's *The Dialogic Imagination* (1981), or some contemporary works on narratology, such as Peter Brook's *Reading for the Plot* (1984), rather than particular studies of her texts. Such theoretical work provides a suggestive and speculative context in which to think about her work.

The study of Jane Austen will always breed problems because one is dealing with a writer who starts with conservative problems and contemplates radical solutions. Hence Rebecca West's remark, in an extraordinarily penetrating Preface to a new edition of *Northanger Abbey* in 1932, 'For the feminism of Jane Austen . . . was very marked. It was, I think, quite conscious', which has remained unnoticed for many years. We stand at a very interesting point in Jane Austen criticism, when rereadings in the light of new forms of thought in the subject are likely to emerge. Jane Austen has recently been well served by historians (Marilyn Butler's *Jane Austen and the War of Ideas*, 1975, re-established the political and intellectual context of the novels), but a great deal more work on the complexities of the politics of the novels is required. Much more feminist history and sustained and careful studies of Jane Austen's language are required. There are signs that this is happening: Elaine Jordan has written seriously of *Lovers' Vows* and Mary Evans has explored the politics of the novels in *Jane Austen and the State* (1987). A computerized study of the language of the novels charts the areas of unease and critical investigation with some subtlety (J. F. Burrows, *Computation into Criticism*, 1987).

Interestingly, Marilyn Butler's *Jane Austen and the War of Ideas*, which argues emphatically for Jane Austen as a conservative writer – Professor Butler describes the first part of *Mansfield Park* in particular as 'a skilful dramatization of the conservative case' – was published in the same year, 1975, as Barbara Hardy's *A Reading of Jane Austen*, which argues a very different case. Professor Hardy cannot read Jane Austen as a conservative and presents her as a novelist who 'criticizes society through the drama of complex and particular types and groups'. Her reading is particularly sensitive to language: she remarks, for instance, on the 'ironic and moral' significance of the 'four inserted words' which open *Mansfield Park* and the description of Sir Thomas's marriage. Maria Ward 'had the good luck to captivate' Sir Thomas Bertram. It is such extreme subtlety of language which makes the conservative reading problematical

by sharply calling attention to the 'luck' of class and money. Her en-
thralling chapter 'Properties and Possessions' likewise shows how the
novels conduct a probing critique of the way people relate to property.

Recently Marilyn Butler has returned to the case for the conservative
reading, prefacing the paperback edition of her book (1987) with a new
and substantial introduction. She reviews her book of 1975, which was
an important moment in Jane Austen criticism, self-critically but un-
apologetically in the light of a comprehensive review of the decade or so
of criticism since, which has seen the rapid growth of very different kinds
of theoretical criticism – feminist criticism, post-structuralist criticism,
deconstruction, psychoanalysis and Marxism. She argues that, as a historical critic, it is still proper for her to maintain her 'conservative'
analysis of 1975. Since she is a critic of very considerable standing who
commands attention, it is worth going into her discussion. She criticizes
feminist accounts of Jane Austen as a 'subversive' as essentially lacking
in historical understanding. Even such impressive works as Elaine Showalter's *A Literature of their Own* (1977) and Susan Gubar and Sandra
Gilbert's *Madwoman in the Attic* (1979) are, she feels, naïve about a
woman's tradition and unscholarly in their readings of the past – or in
their failure to read it. 'Only accurate, comprehensive, particularized
historical criticism, distanced from immediate classroom pressures, willing to take minor work, published and unpublished, male and female, as
evidence, will enable us fully to reconstruct the context in which women
writers wrote' (p. xlv).

But there are more theoretical questions at stake here than Professor
Butler suggests, for what exactly constitutes 'history' is a deeply problematical matter. Isn't 'historical criticism' as much one of the ideological 'classroom pressures' as feminism is? And isn't the dream of the
ultimate and total reconstruction of a historical context a scholar's fan-
tasy? Marilyn Butler writes as if there is only one 'history' to which we
can finally return in all its purity. But there are many histories, and all,
as Hegel realized when he said that history depends on the categories
brought to it by the historian, will be organized through the conceptuali-
zation of history brought to it with the writer of history. We do not have
to fall into a facile relativism to see this. Professor Butler foregrounds
some kinds of history in her book at the expense of others, but this is
inevitable, and the selectiveness gives point to her argument.

No criticism can do without the conceptualizing of history, but
scholars should be warned against the hubris of believing that 'their'
historical methodology is the only one which will lead to a 'correct'
reading. There are many histories: that of language, women, colonial

discourse, for example. And they are often histories of representation and the struggle for representation. Franco Moretti, for instance, has recently seen Jane Austen's work (he discusses *Pride and Prejudice* rather than *Mansfield Park*) in relation to the history of the bourgeois *bildungsroman* of the nineteenth century, in which there is a tension between individual self-development and social normalization, an opposition created by the contradictions of bourgeois values. His 'history' leads to a very different kind of reading of Jane Austen's texts than that pursued by Professor Butler. It is the history of a class morality and aesthetic (*The Way of the World: The* Bildungsroman *in European Culture*, 1987).

But even if one feels one has arrived at the 'right' way of thinking history (and the question is a complex one), there is still a problematical gap between this and the text, which is paradoxically both a part of the 'history' it is in dialogue with and separate from it by the fact of being a fiction. The 'right' history doesn't necessarily guarantee the 'right' reading. For instance, Marilyn Butler sees *Lovers' Vows* as an ideologically questioning intrusion into the novel, which ultimately closes ranks against it and reaffirms conservative values. David Musselwhite, in his *Partings Welded Together: Politics and Desire in the Nineteenth Century Novel* (1987), also sees the response to *Lovers' Vows* as a conservative one, but his reading is entirely different and is, moreover, based on a very different definition of 'conservatism' itself. He argues that the incorporation of the seemingly disruptive *Lovers' Vows* into the novel is a middle-class strategy of appropriation which takes over radical politics and normalizes and tames it.

The terms 'history' and 'conservative', then, turn out to be problematic. A reader of *Mansfield Park* and its contested readings – 'conservative', 'subversive' – has to be a disciplined and meticulous reader of the texts surrounding the novel and the novel itself in order to mediate between opposing interpretations. I believe, however, that it is possible to mediate between these opposing interpretations. To do so involves not so much a historical but a theoretical move. It is possible to recognize the conservative provenance of a writer while understanding the fiction in terms of radical critique. The 'conservative' concern of Southey for the poor, for instance, becomes in the text of *Mansfield Park* a sharper and more complex matter, a questioning of privilege rather more uneasy than that of Southey. The question of what constitutes a historical reading opens up immense problems which cannot be fully discussed here, but one can ask a rather different question of a text: does it open up a space for a radical reading? Some texts do, some do not. In the very anxieties in the text about its own conservative reading, I see the possibilities for radical critique. They are not imposed on it. Marilyn Butler, a critic for whom the greatest respect is appropriate, closes on the conservative reading. It is possible to propose that the conservative reading generates its radical opposition and that this can be seen at many points in the text and above all in the language of the novel. At any rate, this is what my reading has attempted to do.

Within the next decade, perhaps, Jane Austen studies will be taken into new areas. *Mansfield Park*, with its difficult gravitas and sombre perceptions, remains paradoxically the most breathtaking and daring of Jane Austen's novels and will always be a challenge to the critic.

Further Reading

Editions

References are to Kathryn Sutherland's Penguin edition of *Mansfield Park* (1996) because of its availability. R W Chapman's edition of *Mansfield Park*, 1923, is the authoritative work. Chapman also edited *Jane Austen's Letters to her Sister Cassandra and Others*, 1932.

Some Historical Studies

John Barrell, *English Literary History, 1730–80: An Equal, Wide Survey*, 1983.
Ford K. Brown, *Fathers of the Victorians: The Age of Wilberforce*, 1961.
Catherine Gallagher, *The Industrial Reformation*, 1984.
F. M. L. Thompson, *English Landed Society in the Nineteenth Century*, 1963.
Raymond Williams, *The Country and the City*, 1973.

Note: The Penguin edition of William Cobbett's *Rural Rides*, 1967, is also useful as a context for Jane Austen's work.

Studies of Jane Austen

B. C. Southam's *Jane Austen: The Critical Heritage*, 2 vols., 1968, 1987, collects criticism of Jane Austen by major writers and critics from the time of publication of the novels to 1938. The following is a selection from a substantial body of subsequent criticism.

Kingsley Amis, 'What Became of Jane Austen?', *Spectator*, 4 October 1957.
J. F. Burrows, *Computation into Criticism: A Study of Jane Austen's Novels and an Experiment in Method*, 1987.
Marilyn Butler, *Jane Austen and the War of Ideas*, 1975, reprinted with new Introduction, 1987.
D. D. Devlin, *Jane Austen and Education*, 1975.
Alistair M. Duckworth, *The Improvement of the Estate: A Study of Jane Austen's Novels*, 1971.
Mary Evans, *Jane Austen and the State*, 1987.
Avrom Fleishman, *A Reading of* Mansfield Park: *An Essay in Critical Synthesis*, 1967.
Kate Fullbrook, 'Jane Austen and the Comic Negative', in Sue Roe (ed.), *Women Reading Women's Writing*, 1987.
Susan Gubar and Sandra Gilbert, *Madwoman in the Attic*, 1979.

Critical Studies: Mansfield Park

D. W. Harding, 'Regulated Hatred: An Aspect of the Work of Jane Austen', *Scrutiny*, VIII, 1940.

Barbara Hardy, *A Reading of Jane Austen*, 1975.

Park Honan, *Jane Austen: Her Life*, 1987.

Elaine Jordan, 'Pulpit, Stage and Novel: *Mansfield Park* and Mrs Inchbald's *Lovers' Vows*', *Novel*, 20, 1987, pp. 138–48.

Margaret Kirkham, *Jane Austen, Feminism and Fiction*, 1983.

Mary Lascelles, *Jane Austen and Her Art*, 1939.

F. R. Leavis, *The Great Tradition*, 1948.

A. Walton Litz, *Jane Austen: A Study of Her Artistic Development*, 1965.

David Monaghan, *Jane Austen: Structure and Social Vision*, 1980.

Franco Moretti, *The Way of the World: The* Bildungsroman *in European Culture*, 1987.

Marvin Mudrick, *Jane Austen: Irony as Defence and Discovery*, 1952.

David E. Musselwhite, *Partings Welded Together: Politics and Desire in the Nineteenth Century Novel*, 1987.

Jane Nardin, *Those Elegant Decorums: The Concept of Propriety in Jane Austen's Novels*, 1973.

K. C. Phillips, *Jane Austen's English*, 1970.

Warren Roberts, *Jane Austen and the French Revolution*, 1979.

Elaine Showalter, *A Literature of Their Own*, 1977.

Tony Tanner, 'Introduction' to *Mansfield Park*, 1966.

——, *Jane Austen*, 1986.

Lionel Trilling, *The Opposing Self*, 1955.

Theoretical Reading

The reader will often find that speculative writing quite outside an immediate concern with a particular writer will illuminate the work he or she is studying. The following work on aspects of narrative, form, language and ideology might be useful.

*M. M. Bakhtin, *The Dialogic Imagination*, 1981.

*Roland Barthes, *S/Z*, 1974.

——, *Image, Music, Text* (trans. Stephen Heath), 1977.

Peter Brooks, *Reading for the Plot*, 1984.

*Michel Foucault, *The Order of Things* (trans. Tavistock Publications), 1974.

*Gerard Gennett, *Narrative Discourse*, 1980.

Frederic Jameson, *The Political Unconscious: Narrative as a Socially Symbolic Act*, 1981.

*Paul Ricoeur, *Time and Narrative*, 2 vols., 1985.

Shlomith Rimmon-Kenan, *Narrative Fiction: Contemporary Poetics*, 1983.

*Tzvetan Todorov, *The Poetics of Prose*, 1977.

* *Dates given are for translations into English*